Janner's Complete Letterwriter

About the Author

The Hon. Dr Greville Janner QC is Labour MP for Leicester West. A member of the Parliamentary Select Committee on Employment and on Procedure, he is Chairman of the All Party Safety Group.

Dr Janner is President of the Commonwealth Jewish Council and a former President of the Board of Deputies of British Jews. He is married with three children. He speaks eight languages and has made a massive array and variety of speeches and presentations in most parts of the world – from the United States to Australia and from the Far East and Eastern Europe to Egypt and Israel.

Dr Janner, who is a former President of the Cambridge Union, is the only MP who is also a member of the Magic Circle. He is Chairman of Effective Presentational Skills Ltd, a consultancy providing training for all aspects of presentation.

Fourth Edition

Janner's Complete Letterwriter

Greville Janner

Business Books

First published in Great Britain by
Business Books Limited
An imprint of Century Hutchinson Limited
62-65 Chandos Place, London WC2N 4NW

Century Hutchinson Australia (Pty) Limited
89-91 Albion Street, Surry Hills,
New South Wales 2010, Australia

Century Hutchinson New Zealand Limited
PO Box 40-086, 32-34 View Road, Glenfield,
Auckland 10, New Zealand

Century Hutchinson South Africa (Pty) Limited
PO Box 337, Bergvlei 2012, South Africa

First published 1970 under the title
*The Businessman's Guide to Letter-writing
and to the Law of Letters*
Reprinted 1972, 1974
Second edition 1977
Reprinted 1979, 1991 (twice)
Reprinted 1982, 1983 (with new title)
Reprinted
Fourth edition 1989

British Library Cataloguing in Publication Data
Janner, Greville, *1928-*
Janner's complete letterwriter.- 4th ed
1. Letter-writing
I. Title
808.6

ISBN 0-09-173968-3
      0-09-174068-1 Pbk

Printed and bound in Great Britain by
Mackays of Chatham PLC, Chatham, Kent

Dedication

In loving memory of
Emeritus Chief Rabbi Sir Israel Brodie, KBE
and for
Lady Brodie
who taught me that 'respect goes before the law'
with great affection

Contents

Part 4 Letters, for occasions

Part 5 Supplies, systems, staff – and modern techniques

Part 6 Word processing

Part 7 The law on letters

Part 8 Appendices

... be we have not time.

Ever since the last edition, just four years ago, the techniques of word processing have changed and improved. I thank David Roth for updating his invaluable guide to electronic text ... done the best ... chapter ... and tiring automatic process of ...

Introduction

Sam Goldwyn once told an author whose work he had been given to read: 'I read part of it all the way through.' I have now read all of this book, every word and all the way through, and after fifteen years, three editions and innumerable impressions, I discovered that the time had come for an almost complete rewrite.

As a start, I had received a letter from an Australian reader, correctly complaining that the book was clearly written by a man for men. It actually quoted with approval, she pointed out, the saying that in law and literature, 'Man embraces Woman'. He now does not, if he ever did. With the much appreciated assistance of my daughter, Laura, the book has now been written for people.

Next there were too many words and some of them were incomprehensible. As Will Rogers remarked: 'The minute that you read something that you can't understand, you can almost be sure it was drawn up by a lawyer.' It was, but it should not have shown and I hope it no longer does.

Which leads to the third change. I have pared down and combined the chapters on the law in letters, and on letters in litigation. The essentials remain, carefully and, I hope, clearly set out.

In a sense, Goldwyn was right. Books of this sort are for dipping into and for reference, as well as for relaxed and prolonged reading. So we have a new index.

Even since the last edition, just four years ago, the techniques of word processing have changed and improved. I thank David Roth for updating his invaluable guide, explaining as it does the basics of choosing and using automatic processing for letter-writing.

Letter posting and the services of the Post Office remain in Appendix 1. I thank Nina Cooper for updating it.

The essentials of the work remain. I hope that it will continue as the standard definitive guide to the letterwriter's art. It is the product of over forty years of practical letter-writing – professional and personal, organizational and social, legal and general. I hope it will give you pleasure and help.

Finally, my thanks to my colleague, Leslie Benson; to my wife, Myra; and to my patient secretaries, Pat Garner and Margaret Lancaster, for all their help in preparing this new edition.

Greville Janner
London
1989

For details of audio-manuals, in-company training in presentational skills and employment law, contact: Paul Secher LL.B, J.S. Associates 8 Balfour Place, London W1Y 5RS; tel: 01-408 2063.

Part 1

FORM AND FORMALITIES

'Dear Madame,

You may wonder why I'm demanding money from you under the threat of violence. Perhaps a few words about myself will help explain matters. I was born to a middle-class family forty-two years ago . . . .

Yours most sincerely . . .'

1

The shape of a letter

A fine letter must have form and shape. For ordinary, simple notes;
this creates little worry. By the time you have kicked off with 'Thank
you for your letter ...' and ended with 'Kindest regards', the middle
will have looked after itself. But when a letter is important; when it
matters to you; when you are prepared to take time to work on the
words – then you should divide your draft into three parts: the
opening, the body and the closing. Create the skeleton in note form;
clothe it with the ideas you want to put across; and so the letter takes
shape. As with a structured speech or any other presentation, say
what you are going to say; say it; then say what you've said.

The first and last sentences are crucial. Skip the traditional
opening gambit ('We are in receipt of ...'). Start with a clear first
sentence, to catch the reader's interest, to sum up what is to come,
and to make sure that your words will be taken seriously.

Next, each idea should lead on logically to the next. Just as each
bone of the human body is attached to its fellow, so the ideas in a
letter should be jointed. The flow of ideas needs rhythm. Disjointed
ideas, dislocated thoughts, fractured theories, these are the hallmarks of a poor and ineffective missive.

So jot down the points you need to make. Then set them out in
logical order, so that one flows on to the next. Connect them up, if
you like, with a general theme. Start with the theme; elaborate, point
by point; then round off with the punch line or message. Explain
what action should follow.

A good, sound ending to a well-constructed letter should bring
business or whatever other results you seek. If the skeleton of the
letter is sound, then even if the body is not as strong as it might be, the
reader may not notice.

It was said of the great eighteenth century lawyer, Sir William
Blackstone: 'He it was that first gave the law the air of a science. He

found it a skeleton and clothed it with life, colour and complexion; he embraced the cold statue and by his touch it grew into youth, health and beauty.'

You do not start with the letter of the law – you take the skeleton and you flesh it out. Create that foundation and clothe it with 'life, colour and complexion'.

2

Hail and farewell – the start and finish of a letter

A poor beginning or an inadequate end spoils any letter. Happily, the formalities dictated by usage and etiquette do much to ease the writer's path – if they are used correctly.

However much you may dislike the recipient of your letter, there is seldom any alternative to using 'Dear'. 'Hated Sir' might be a splendid thought, but to leave out the 'Dear' altogether is about as far as hostility (or formality) can decently go. Generally, such an opening denotes hostility implacable, indignation unquenchable. It has a Victorian ring and should seldom be used, except in rare official (probably governmental) and traditional notifications.

The use of a person's name without the opening endearment is generally only suitable for inter-office memos – or for deliberately offensive letters written (perhaps) to ex-partners or associates: 'Jackson: I can no longer endure working with you ...'

What really matters is to get the name right. If you do not take the trouble to find out the spelling of your correspondents' surnames, you can scarcely blame them if they feel that you are not really concerned with their business. We are all inordinately sensitive about our names. They represent ourselves. Not for nothing do political ruffians disfigure the names of their enemies on signs, posters and hoardings.

To make an error in a person's name is normally a sign of nothing but carelessness, which itself is hardly a good advertisement for you, your wares or your services. If in doubt check. A telephone call to the recipient's secretary (or even telephonist) would put things right. Is his name Philip with one 'l' or two? is she 'Goldsmith' or 'Goldsmidt' or, for that matter 'Goldschmidt'? is he 'Mr Ewan Richard' or 'Mr Evan Richards', 'Mr Harald Stewart' or 'Mr Harold Stuart'?

When writing to a woman, try to address her correctly and as she would wish – as 'Mrs' or 'Miss' or 'Ms'. Some women see no reason why their marital status should be revealed in their form of address, any more than it is for a man. 'Ms' is an accepted modern form of address.

Of course 'Dear Madam' (with an 'e' at the end only when writing to a French woman, to the wife of an ambassador or possibly to a brothel proprietress) solves the problem, in the same way as 'Dear Sir' or 'Dear Sirs'. It is a very formal approach, and should generally be reserved for strictly formal letters, including those written to public bodies as such, as opposed to specific individuals within them. If you wish to deal with a person on a personal basis, then use his or her name.

Whether or not to address people by their first (or 'given' or Christian) names is usually a matter of tact, dependent on your acquaintance or friendship with them. It is often a mistake to be too chummy, but if you can get on first-name terms with business contacts then (in most cases) it will help to lower the fences between you. There are other occasions, however, when keeping your distance may be an advantage. You must judge each occasion, problem and recipient for yourself.

What, then, of the word 'my': 'My dear James' or 'My dear Mrs Brown'?

Use this approach with care. An upper-crust indication of warmth, it is sometimes taken by others to imply condescension. Customs differ, but if in doubt, leave off the 'my'.

When you have addressed the recipient by his or her own name (surname or first name, as the case may be), you should almost invariably finish with 'Yours sincerely'. 'Yours very sincerely' is in order, if a little flowery. 'Yours ever' should be reserved for friends. 'Yours truly' is a handy variation used where the recipient is not well known to the writer.

'Yours faithfully' is the appropriate ending to a letter which begins 'Dear Sir'. It has replaced the old-fashioned 'I remain, your obedient servant', even in military letters.

The order of the final words is sometimes reversed, but this is usually an affectation. 'Faithfully yours' or 'Very sincerely yours' are rarities. Between friends 'Yours' on its own is common. 'As ever' or 'Yours ever' do good service. 'Sincerely' adds a touch of goodwill. But all these are variations on the basic themes of 'Dear Sir ... Yours faithfully' and 'Dear Mrs Brown ... Yours sincerely'.

So stick to the formalities and you are likely to start and finish correctly. You can then concentrate on the body of the letter.

3

Signatures and postscripts

There are people who make their living by interpreting character as expressed in signatures. Loops, whirls and lines, we are told, all have hidden meanings. Slope the words downwards and you are likely to be depressed and pessimistic; slope them up and the graphologist recognises an extroverted optimist. Whether this has any scientific foundation is arguable (and often argued). But the importance of a sensible signature is indisputable.

Your signature is your symbol. How do you make it? The height of modesty is to use an initial only: 'N. Smith'. Next in the scale of self-assertion, the forename and surname: 'Norman Smith'. Then comes the extra initial: 'Norman H. Smith'. Finally and most flourishing: 'Norman Halliwell Smith'.

Which signature will impress most depends on the nature of the letter. Suppose, for instance, the writer wants a job as a salesman. The more extroverted he manages to appear, the more likely it is that he will get the post. Conversely, if a director is seeking a self-effacing assistant, he should look for someone with the quiet initials.

Finally, if you have to sign dozens of letters a day, you should develop a characteristic scrawl, to give your imprimatur with the minimum expenditure of time and effort. But a self-assured and swift symbol which impresses your staff or your regular correspondents may be counter-productive if the recipient expects to be treated with careful, considered respect. If you received an application for an executive position signed with a swirl and a squiggle, would you be impressed? Hardly.

One prominent executive may often be heard to say, 'A business-man's mind should be like a chemist's shop: a place for everything and everything in its place,' or, 'A tidy mind in a tidy body – that is the recipe for success.' If a signature is slovenly, then (rightly or wrongly) its reader may draw the obvious conclusion about the signatory.

Traders and merchants once took great pride in their seals. If they needed to sign, they pressed their ring or sealing rod or cylinder onto the wax and made their mark. Today, alas, the handsome, chiselled seal is gone. The only exceptions I know are the prime ministers of India.

Your mark is your signature. It puts the final touch to your letters. So ensure that the touch is firm, appropriate and impressive. Many a good letter brings bad results because the writer is too lazy or thoughtless to add a fine, smart signature, suited to the nature and design of the words it rounds off.

Before you sign your letter, do make sure that it includes everything that you have in mind. A PS may help, but it may also make afterthoughts too obvious. In sales letters, though, the first sentence and the PS are the most likely to be read.

Omissions may be corrected either by rewriting of the letter itself, or by a typed or handwritten PS. Anything of potential importance should also be transposed to the copy. So spare time to read your letters, quietly and carefully, before you sign them.

There is nothing wrong in getting your secretary to put at the foot: 'Dictated by Mr James Jones but signed in his absence', or simply: 'Diane Williams, pp James Jones'. Provided your correspondent will not be offended, all is well. But do make certain that the words for which you will be held responsible are accurate. You might even say: 'I hope that you will not mind this letter being signed in my absence by my secretary, so as to save a day – I am away tomorrow'.

If this happens often, then why not invest in a battery of those excellent stamps which give your secretary the choice between the different forms of 'pp' signatures. But be warned: please do not, repeat *not*, allow your secretary or anyone else to sign a letter on your behalf without your approval – other than in the rarest cases and when you have the most reliable pro-signatory.

Robert Browning, praising the glories of England in April, extolled 'the wise thrush; he sings each song twice over'. Wise letterwriters read the contents at least once over, with care. Far too many letters are sent unread, with a hastily-scrawled signature.

4

Lists and schedules

Essentially, a letter is a vehicle for ideas. Dry facts are better in an enclosure or appendix.

In general, a letter is meant to be read. If the recipient is too bored or aggravated to read it to the end – because it has been carelessly drafted, poorly written, badly typed, or is simply inept, inadequate or unfit for its purpose – then it has failed in its objective.

Lists or schedules are (usually, at least) intended to be consulted, perused, dipped into or extracted from, but unless the accompanying letter is apt, the list or schedule will be useless. Letters sell their writers' ideas, and often their goods or services. So do schedules and enclosures, so treat them too with respect. If you want your enclosures to bear good fruit, fertilize them with your time, care and consideration. You have no time to spare? Then make sure that someone else does so for you. Your enclosures should neither be, nor appear, as afterthoughts.

Some lists fit well into the body of the letter. If you are setting out a string of thoughts, then number them. Thus:

Our reasons are the following:

(1) The product is too new.
(2) The area is too limited.
(3) ...
    Alternatively:

We are sure that you will appreciate the reductions in price in the following products:

(1) ...
and so on.

Lists can make a letter live. If you pack your facts or arguments all together into a paragraph you may succeed only in confusing both the opposition and yourself. List your thoughts, and if on reading them through you notice that logic is missing then *you* will know that you must redraft your letter, recast your list or change your mind accordingly.

Do remember to refer to the enclosure not only in the letter itself but also at its foot. The word 'enclosure' (or 'enc.') should do the trick. Or staple the letter to the accompanying documents so that they cannot go adrift. For every letter that gets lost, there must be fifty missing enclosures – which means a loss to the writer and aggravation for the recipient. Make sure that both letter and enclosure are sent, and that they stick together.

In 'How to Write Short Stories', Ring Lardner advised: 'A good many young writers make the mistake of enclosing a stamped, self-addressed envelope, big enough for the manuscript to come back in. This is too much temptation for the editor.'

Use stamped, addressed envelopes and all other enclosures with discretion. Are they what you want? Are they really necessary? And are they there?

5

References – on letters

References are as important for letters as they are for people. Careful, sensible, thoughtful referencing saves work, time and money. It informs the recipient immediately of the subject of your letter. It avoids mistakes and shows that you are a courteous correspondent. It also helps your own filing system to operate efficiently.

Every business letter should bear a general reference, after the opening or at the top of the page.

> Dear Sir,
> Your order no. 25873

Or:

> Dear Sir,
> Directors' Loan Account

If you initiate the correspondence, you can generally choose the main reference. Try to make it specific. Where possible, for instance, refer to an order or contract by a number, and to people by their full name rather than by surname alone. The more precise your reference, the greater its usefulness.

If the correspondence is started by another party you will have their reference which you should repeat on your reply. But do not hesitate to add a reference of your own.

As well as the subject matter, the general reference should also indicate the identity of both the writer and the secretary or typist. There are two ways of doing this. It is usual to include the initials of each person. But if you would rather remain anonymous, you can allocate numbers or letters to every executive, partner and member of staff. If anyone wants to find out the identity of someone whose initials are on the notepaper, they can telephone the business number and ask. Where the letter is deliberately anonymous (as in some debt-collecting missives) it may be preferable to include a reference which is clear to you but meaningless to your correspondents.

Obviously, copies of all important corespondence will be kept and filed (see Chapter 45). The filing may be done by a highly trained secretary, which would probably be a waste of good and expensive time. More likely you will employ a filing clerk, or put office juniors onto the filing chore as part of their daily routine. You must then recognize the limitations of your employees, and allow for them. If you want copies to be readily available, they must appear on the right file.

Your referencing must therefore be precise, clear and individual. So why not spare a few minutes of careful thought now, to avoid wasting time and energy in future?

6

The layout

Well-marshalled thoughts expressed in well-chosen words may still convey the wrong impression if the letter is carelessly laid out. So instruct your secretary and typists in the layout you require.

You may decide on some special house style. Eccentricity may be in your line. There are millionaires who slouch around in baggy trousers, multi-coloured neckties and without a penny in their pockets. I treasure letters from a great foreign statesman containing torrents of thought, poured out on the scruffiest of paper and entirely without paragraphs. The mighty are entitled to their foibles.

For the average successful executive – and for anyone who aspires to even higher levels in the commerical world – more prosaic behaviour is advisable. Once you are chairman, if your fingernails are dirty this may perhaps be regarded as one of the unworthy but forgivable ways of 'the Old Man', who has better things to do than to attend to his toilet. If you are the majority shareholder as well as managing director, then your notepaper may be scruffy, and too bad if anyone minds. If you are lower down the line, or if you wish to stay at the top of the heap, appearances matter.

Executives generally realize the importance of being well groomed. They may even appreciate that their stationery should be as well turned out as they are. It is remarkable, though, how many people at the top take too little care about the layout of their letters.

Eccentricities apart, we recommend a standard style. Across the top of the letter goes your heading. On one side (it matters not which) comes your address. Slightly lower down, and preferably on the opposite side, you put the recipient's address. The date goes where it balances best.

Then 'Dear Sir' (or as the case may be) goes hard against the left margin. Next comes the reference. Margins on each side should be big enough to create a sense of space and to allow for the recipient's notes.

Lines should be double-spaced, with treble-spacing between paragraphs – which should be indented. Sub-paragraphs need further indentation. Finally, the sign-off comes towards the middle of the page. Leave enough space for the signature. Underneath comes the name of the writer, and underneath that his or her style or position.

If there are enclosures, add 'enclosure' (or the abbreviation 'enc.') in a bottom corner (see Chapter 4). If your letter will not fit on one page, use a continuation sheet rather than the back of the paper. All stationery should be ordered with continuation sheets of identical paper in the same size.

Here is a simple suggested layout:

The Jamestown plc
24 High Street, Jamesville, Beds

Ref: GJ23   1 July 1988

Roger Brown & Co. Ltd
38 Upper Street,
Millbury, Wilts.

Dear Sirs,

We thank you for your letter of 30 August. We shall be pleased to supply the goods required, if you will kindly provide the following further information:

   (a)
   (b)
   (c)

We look forward to an early reply and will do our best to despatch the goods immediately we receive your further instructions.

Yours faithfully,

Director

7

Acknowledgments – and standard forms*

The surest way to lose friends and influence is not to reply to their letters.

Part of the art of ensuring prompt replies lies in an efficient office system. Are you satisfied that yours is as good as you can make it? Is incoming mail stamped with a date and shipped off smartly to the appropriate department? Do letters requiring an immediate answer always get one? If there is to be delay, is the appropriate acknowledgment sent?

For instance, 'We thank you for your letter of ... which is receiving attention' or 'Thank you for your order. We shall deal with this as soon as possible' or 'Your communication is acknowledged. A reply will be sent shortly' or 'Thank you for your letter of ... This has been passed to ... for his attention.'

What you really need is a batch of assorted acknowledgments, to be sent out as required. The person who sorts out the mail should be able to decide which acknowledgment would be best, and then put each letter in the appropriate tray, or say to a secretary, 'Form 1 for this, please ... Form 2 for that ...'

Standard forms there must be. These can be simple, brief, and on postcards. Or you may need something lengthier. For example, you may want to set out a series of possible common answers to a communication, all but one or two of which can be crossed out, for example:

> We regret that we have not received the order to which you refer.
> Would you please send a copy so that the matter may be dealt with as quickly as possible.

*See also Part 6 on word processing.

We thank you for your order, but you do not give an address for delivery. Please do so, and the goods will be despatched within ...days/weeks/ months.

We regret that it is not possible to despatch orders overseas.

We regret that the lines which you have ordered are for export only. We are sorry that we cannot be of assistance on this occasion.

The goods of your order have been sent to you by post/air/sea. They should reach you by about ... If they are not received by then, kindly contact us again.

We have checked our records. These indicate that the goods were despatched to you on ... We regret that they appear to have been lost in the post. We will send replacements without extra charge/investigate the matter/contact our carriers forthwith.

Unfortunately, we are not able to open accounts for small amounts. If you will kindly send a cheque or postal order, we shall despatch at once.

You may add a standard PS: 'We have pleasure in enclosing our latest catalogue, which we hope will be of interest to you' or 'In case our other products may be of interest to you, we shall shortly be sending an up-to-date catalogue and price list' or 'It has been a pleasure to do business with you. We shall send you further details of new lines.'

It is, of course, important that even *pro forma* letters should be well laid out (see Chapter 6), and properly produced. You may have facilities for printing on your premises or you may decide to use a duplicating machine.

There is a tremendous and growing variety of magnificent reproduction machinery on the market, tailored to suit almost every commercial pocket (details in Part 6). Before you buy or rent make sure that servicing and spares will be readily available.

Keep your eyes on the journals aimed at potential buyers (and often sent on a controlled circulation basis). If you are not on the various mailing lists, ask your secretary to make a few phone calls and get yourself added. For details of current publications you could look at the *Annual Press Directory*, which is in every comprehensive reference library. Or ask your business friends to pass over the journals they get.

Of course, the nature and number of the forms which you should have in stock will vary according to your business. You may find it helpful to prepare a variety of forms, to be adapted. Your word processor will cope.

Organize your letter-writing system carefully. Work out which letters can be reprodeced, by whatever method is most appropriate.

Set on one side those which are standard enough to use draft precedents, and use them to lean on. If you do not want to invest in a collection of other people's drafts, then prepare one of your own. And leave for individual drafting only those letters which need special thought and attention.

8
Titles

The most common title (apart from a military or police rank) is 'Sir'. This is accorded to knights and baronets of various orders and degrees. In each case, unless you are on first-name terms with them, the correct form of address is 'Dear Sir Arthur', 'Dear Sir Barnett' or as the case may be. But never 'Dear Sir Jones'.

To the wife of a knight or a Baronet you write 'Dear Jane' if you know her well enough, or otherwise 'Dear Lady Jones'. The same applies if she is the wife of Lord Jones.

If the lady has a title in her own right, then you also address her as 'Dear Lady Jones' or (if she is a life peeress) 'Dear Baroness Jones'. Or if you are on friendly but not first-name terms, 'My dear Baroness' or 'Dear Baroness'.

The exception to this use of the surname for ladies is the daughter of a viscount, earl, marquis or duke. She is accorded the courtesy title of 'Lady Jane Jones' – so you write to her as 'Dear Lady Jane'.

The children of all peers (life or hereditary) have the courtesy title of 'The Honourable'. But you still write to them as 'Dear Mr ...' or 'Dear John', and never as 'Dear Honourable Jones'. As the son of a peer I receive many letters, often computerized, starting (in Japanese fashion), 'Dear Honourable Greville'.

The woman with the female equivalent of a knighthood is a dame. She is not addressed as 'Lady' but as 'Dame', and with a knight, the title is combined with the first name and not her surname. Hence, 'Dear Dame Jane' and *not* 'Dear Dame Jones'.

The highest rank before the peerage is a baronet. On the envelope he is called: 'Sir James Jones, Bt' – but the 'Bt' is never used when addressing the gentleman. Equally, the lowest rank of the peerage is a baron. While, as we have seen, baronesses are often addressed by their title, the same does not apply to barons. They are always called 'Lord'. Hence: 'Dear Lord Jones'.

Higher up the lordly scale you may write 'Dear Viscount Jones' or 'Dear Lord Jones' – either would do. The same applies to earls, marquises and dukes.

The wife of a duke is a duchess; of a marquis, a marchioness; of an earl, a countess; of a viscount, a viscountess. Write to them as either: 'Dear Lady Jones' or 'Dear Countess Jones' – but just as you write to a duke as 'Your Grace', the same dignity is accorded to his wife. Never write 'Dear Duchess Jones'.

What, then, of priests and ministers of religion? 'Dear Reverend Green'; 'Dear Father Green'; 'Dear Monsignor Green'; or 'Dear Rabbi Green' – all these are fine. For Archbishop Green: 'Dear Archbishop' (informally) or 'Your Grace' (formally).

The formal sign-off should nowadays be simply 'Yours faithfully', 'Yours truly' or 'Yours sincerely'.

Archbishops are generally addressed as 'His Grace the Lord Archbishop of ...'. Address a bishop as 'The Right Reverend the Lord Bishop of ...' or 'The Lord Bishop of ...', and start your letter 'My Lord Bishop' or 'Your Lordship'. Or, if you know him, but not well enough for first names, 'Dear Bishop'.

Catholic dignitaries generally receive the same courtesies as their Protestant brethren. The following guide is suggested: When writing to a Cardinal, address the envelope 'His Eminence the Cardinal Archbishop of ...', and start the letter with 'Your Eminence' or 'My Lord Cardinal'. Address a Catholic bishop as 'His Lordship the Bishop of ...' and start 'My Lord'. Address a Catholic priest as 'The Reverend ...' and start the letter 'Dear Father ...'.

The Chief Rabbi should be addressed as 'The Very Reverend the Chief Rabbi'. Start your letter: 'Dear Chief Rabbi'. Otherwise, address rabbis as 'Rabbi Michael Cohen', or 'Rabbi Dr Michael Cohen' (as the case may be), and 'Dear Rabbi Cohen'. A Jewish minister who does not hold a rabbinical diploma is normally 'The Reverend Michael Cohen'. Start 'Dear Reverend Cohen' or 'Dear Mr Cohen'.

Now the law. If you know a judge well use his or her first name. If you know him or her reasonably well (but you are not on first-name terms), address him or her as 'Sir William' or 'Lady Jane' or 'Dame' or 'Judge Jones' (according to rank).

Writing to the Lord Chancellor? Address the envelope to 'The Right Honourable The Lord Chancellor' and start 'My Lord' or 'Dear Lord Chancellor'. The same style is appropriate for Lords of Appeal in Ordinary and the Lord Chief Justice.

Address the Master of the Rolls as 'The Right Honourable Lord ...', 'The Right Honourable Sir ... Master of the Rolls', or 'His Honour, The Master of the Rolls'.

Lord Justices of Appeal? Address them as 'The Rt Hon. the Lord Justice ...', or 'The Rt Hon. Sir William..., Lord Justice of Appeal', and start 'Dear Sir' or 'Dear Sir William'.

Lord Mayors? 'The Right Honourable The Lord Mayor of ...', followed by 'My Lord ...'. An ordinary mayor is 'His (or Her) Worship, the Mayor of ...', followed by 'Your Worship ...'.

Address a Member of Parliament as 'Hilary Smith, MP', or, if he or she is a Privy Councillor, 'the Rt Hon. Hilary Smith, MP'. In either case, start 'Dear Sir' or 'Dear Madam' or 'Dear Mr (or Mrs) Smith'.

Doctors of medicine should be addressed as 'Dr Roger Smith', except surgeons, who are 'Mr'. Hence, 'Roger Smith, FRCS ... Dear Mr Smith ...'.

Address a commissioned officer in one of the armed services by rank, together with decorations if any. To a Lieutenant-Colonel write 'Dear Colonel ...' and never 'Dear Lt-Col ...'. You may add the arm of service to the title of army officers and 'RN' to the address of naval officers.

Some say that when a letter is meant for more than one person, it should be addressed to only one of them. But 'Dear Mr and Mrs Jones' is much better. Leave out their degrees and the like. If you write to Sir James Smith, MP alone, all is well, but omit the MP when writing to Sir James and Lady Smith. Or you could write to Sir James Smith MP and Lady Smith JP, for instance.

If you are addressing two or more people other than husband and wife, use both their names: 'Mr Roger Brown and Ms Jane White', or 'Mrs Mary Green and Mrs Dorothy Red.'

What of 'Esquire', or 'Esq.'? Esquires were the rank below knights. The title was properly accorded to barristers and other presumed gentlemen, and by courtesy (or for the sake of flattery) to all men. It is now unnecessary and on its way out.

And 'Master John Smith' for a child? Gone, along with my childhood: John Smith will do fine.

These are general rules. If in doubt, get your secretary to telephone. 'How does the M.D. like to be addressed, please?' You will soon find the answer and avoid unnecessary irritation. People are touchy about their title and form of address. Courtesy requires you to address your correspondent with all due care.

Part 2

STYLE AND GRAMMAR

'Pretty stylish set of references I have there, eh Mr. Bradley?'

9

Style

You judge applicants for a job by their clothes, appearance and manner of speech or writing – in a word, by their style. First impressions may be vital, so style is crucial. If you get to know an applicant other factors come into play – character and intellect, in particular. But at first it is outward style that matters. If that is poor, then you may never discover that a gauche exterior conceals a mind of worth.

Equally, letterwriters should recognize the immediate impact of their correspondence. This means paying careful attention to stationery and printing (Chapter 45), to cleanness of type and to the skills of typists or secretaries (see Chapter 53) and, above all, to the words themselves.

Grammar matters (see Chapter 10). If the writer is uneducated, unless precedents are used and adapted with loving care, the reader will know.

The best and most permanent answer is for the writer to become a reader. Do you take pride in your library? The first stage in correction is recognition of failings. If you can achieve this on your own, fine. But why is there such a prejudice among business people against formal education in letterwriting and literature generally?

Style cannot, of course, be detached from general layout. The letterwriter, like the athlete, must get the start and finish just right if he is to produce a winner. The content must be clear, brief, lucid and pleasantly paragraphed (Chapter 12). Above all, the style of the words must reflect the intention of the letter.

What do you wear when you greet an executive from abroad? Dress must suit the occasion or it may cause embarrassment, upset, or loss of business. The words of the letterwriter are the dress of thought. If they are inept, slovenly or ill-suited to the occasion their style will destroy their impact. So fit style to circumstance.

Somerset Maugham said: 'A good style should show no sign of effort. What is written should seem a happy accident.' To put it in the words of Samuel Johnson (quoting a college tutor): 'Read over your compositions and wherever you meet with a passage which you think is particularly fine, strike it out'.

Grammatical thoughts, ungrammatical words – and adult remedies

'Between you and I', the letter begins – and if the reader is a purist, there the correspondence ends. If the writer is applying for a job, prospects pall. Instead of achieving a confidential approach, the applicant has revealed an ignorance of elementary English grammar.

Another common mistake: 'I am obliged to you for the courtesy extended to Mr Brown and I on our recent visit to your factory.' Courtesy extended to I?

'My staff and me are grateful ...' So 'me' is grateful, is me? Someone does not understand the use of the accusative, and is guilty of a very common linguistic crime.

When you write letters, your accent disappears. Your speech may bear the marks of Belgravia or Bohemia, Brooklyn or Bermondsey, but your writing receives no overtones from your voice.

This may be an asset, for an accent is not always an advantage. But on paper everyone starts on the same level. Pens and word processors are classless instruments. The heavily accented words which you speak into your dictating machine emerge classless, sexless and without any indication of ethnic origin. At least, they should.

In practice, grammar is the giveaway. It places the seal of education on the letter of authority. Conversely, if he or she expresses himself ungrammatically, the writer stands revealed as uneducated. Not for nothing do we use the words 'unlettered' and 'illiterate' for those whose education is lacking.

We do not all receive the same opportunities in our early years. Some top tycoons were forced into the business world at an early age. Once there, however, many read widely and improved themselves. Good companies buy good books if they wish to have excellent executives.

How can you repair broken English? Here are three suggestions. First, read well and widely. By all means study the financial columns in the newspapers and the form of both companies and horses. But fill in those longer periods on the train or the bus, in the car or the taxi, by reading something more profound. Have you dipped into Hersey or Hemmingway? Do you really think that David Copperfield was only a character in a film? Have you relived those memorable wartime years in the words of Winston Churchill? What of Solzhenitsyn, or the latest winner of the Booker prize?

Schools too often spell 'literature' with a capital 'L'. They destroy young people's appetite for Shakespeare by turning his words into examination fodder. This is a pity. To write well you should read widely. The greater your failings as a grammarian, the more you should marinate your mind in the rich wine of fine literature. Letterwriters who wish their words to have impact should read the letters of others. Many people have consigned their thoughts to letters. Some have caused or permitted their letters to be published. Read them.

Second, listen to good speeches. When you are hear the language well spoken, make a note. To copy the excellent is a mark of wisdom, provided only that you do not breach the laws of copyright (Chapter 51).

Finally, do not turn up your nose at formal courses aimed at adults. If you do not want to attend a class, then have one custommade. Find yourself a teacher. The money will be well spent. Or try a correspondence course: there are plenty about. Bear the cost or get your employer to do so. It pays to learn and it is never too late to polish up your language.

11

Punctuation, self-expression – and the limits to formal grammar

The object of most letters is to promote ideas. Whether you are buying or selling, hiring or firing, praising, decrying, apologising or negotiating, matters not. You are expressing yourself on paper. As we shall see in Chapter 16, there are occasions when formality helps to keep the self hidden. Generally, though, say what you must (or what you wish) with clarity. And express your personality with your views.

We are told at school that sentences must have verbs. Not necessarily. A sentence usually has a verb. Not always. Grammar has its place, but there is also room for the thrusting, vivid expression of informal thought.

Do not fear the lively phrase. Words may make a sentence with no verb. So may one word, on its own. Often. And effectively.

In general, sentences should not begin with 'And' or 'But'. But they often do. And to good effect. You are the writer. You make your rules. Yours is the meaning to be expressed, the personality to be put across; your style is for you to choose.

Take punctuation. 'Period' is the pungent American name for the full stop. It indicates a break in thought. A comma marks a pause. A semicolon is half a colon and is useful for indicating the end of an item in a list. The colon comes between the semicolon and the full stop: we have a pause in the flow of thought, but not for long.

The dash is a useful weapon – it indicates the break in the sentence (or list) longer than that signified by a series of dots ... These show that the thought has not ended, even though the sentence or the paragraph may have.

Careful punctuation breaks up a paragraph or a sentence. The breezier the style you choose, the more you will make of the dot and the dash.

Suiting the style to the subject and to the writer is more important even than the careful choice of words.

Modern usage often justifies the ignoring of old rules. Take the split infinitive, for example. I hate it, but that is a matter of taste. 'To carefully fix' 'to gently remind', 'to kindly honour' 'to swiftly reply', 'to eagerly await', 'to please reply': these are all quite common. But we all have our linguistic foibles, and I cringe at the splitting of the infinitive for any purpose. My views on this may be old-fashioned. Before you split infinitives in your letters, though, do bear in mind that the recipient of your letter – perhaps an important customer (actual or potential) or someone else whom you wish to please – may be as wrong, old-fashioned and stupid as I am.

In the margin of a state document, Winston Churchill once wrote, 'This is the sort of English up with which I will not put'.

You must carefully tread the path between precision and pedantry.

12

Brevity

Those of us who are small in physical stature are often reassured by kindly friends who say: 'The best things come in small packages ... A little person is a beautiful thing ... It's the size of the brain that counts ...' and so on.

For the man who craves those extra inches in order to dominate an audience, for the woman who regularly has to speak in public while resting her chin on the table, these thoughts provide little consolation. But they do contain a germ of truth. Length is fine in its way, but it may be a nuisance. Tall people cannot stretch out in the bath or extend their legs in a sleeper or couchette. They can peer over the top of the crowd but seldom slide through it. As with people, so with letters.

There are times when a letter must be long to achieve its purpose. But generally, the shorter the words, the sentences and the letter, the more effective the results will be. Even the longest epistle should be broken up into brief sections. There is no excuse for the sentence that stretches into a paragraph, nor the paragraph that becomes a page.

Brevity is the soul of a good letter. Short, snappy, concise, clear and pungent paragraphs. Thoughts neatly packed into words with punch. Neat, lively expressions, shorn of padding and pomposity. These are the keys to successful correspondence.

The bore, the windbag, the person whom we would all go the longest distance to avoid, is also the writer whose letters we least like to read. 'Oh, him again,' you say, recognizing the prolix prose. 'I'll read it later ... if I have time.' So the writer joins the ranks of the great unread.

In the world of journalism there are newspapers that pay by the word or column inch. This puts a premium on padding. Many professional writers (like me) do their best to avoid this sort of yardstick. 'We only want 500 words' writes the editor. 'We pay £x per thousand.' 'I shall be delighted to write your piece!' the journalist replies. 'But it will be harder for me to condense the material you want into 500 words than to produce a piece of 1,000. I suggest that it would be fairer to pay the rate of £x for the 500-word piece. It will take me longer to write and will cost more in care.' With luck, the editor will agree – as a professional, he will know that length and value are seldom the same. Quality counts. Brevity matters.

Churchill was once asked how long it took him to prepare a speech. 'If it's a two-hour speech,' he replied 'ten minutes. If it's a ten-minute speech, two hours.'

In the world of public speaking there is a trite saying: 'Stand up, speak up and then shut up'. But at least the spoken word is transitory. Unless you are on radio or television, or you are a politician who produces some glorious gaffe – or, of course, you slander someone – your words will probably go unrecorded and unremembered. Commercial correspondents, though, have their words preserved in files, to be used in evidence if necessary. So keep those words short, accurate and to the point.

If you find that your letter is too long, take out your equivalent of the sub-editor's blue pencil. Peel away the extra words with which your thoughts are clothed and leave them to stand on their own naked merits. If you are ashamed of them when they stand stripped then think again. Redraft, rewrite, rethink ... Excess verbiage not only offends, bores and muddles the reader. It also fools the writer.

When General Eisenhower appointed Arthur Burns as Chairman of his Economic Advisors, Burns suggested sending the President a memo outlining plans to organize the flow of economic advice. Ike said, 'Keep it short. I can't read.' Burns replied, 'That's fine, Mr President. I can't write!' So they had a one-hour weekly conference instead.

A magazine once asked millionaire Paul Getty for a short article explaining his success. The editor enclosed his cheque for £200. The multi-millionaire wrote: 'Some people find oil. Others don't.'

Be brief, then. Or in the famous words of another oil man, 'If you don't strike oil soon, stop boring!'

13

The choice of words – and words to the wise

Businesses succeed or fail according to someone's choice of personnel. Two of the best ways of assessing people's calibre are by looking at their taste in friends and in books. Authors or speakers make their impact through the words they use and the way they use them.

Consider, first, how one person's attitude may be described in many ways, some approving, some definitely not. Suppose that your correspondent refuses to budge from a point of view. You may describe him or her as stubborn or stiff-necked, mulish, pig-headed, intractable, obdurate, hardline or intransigent, fanatical or thick. Clearly you disapprove.

You could equally well call them: dogged, pertinacious, determined, resolute, steady, constant, reliable: in other words, this person is courageous, and can be trusted. He or she will not bend before every blast, or trim their sales to even the strongest wind (splendid clichés those – see Chapter 15).

So, adjectives must be handled with particular care. Meaning is fragile and may shatter if struck by the wrong expression.

But finding the right word (or the *mot juste* – the word which will do justice to the occasion) may be a difficult task. 'I can't put my finger on the expression I want. What was the word for that? Oh, never mind,' says the letterwriter, using whatever expression comes to mind.

'What else was he to do?' you ask. Well, he could ask someone else to pin down the word for him. Or he could consult that great work *Roget's Thesaurus*. Here are tens of thousands of words, sorted into categories, with synonyms and antonyms, verbs and adjectives, nouns, pronouns – the lot. It costs little and is available in hard cover or paperback. Every writer and speaker should keep it handy.

You also need a dictionary. It makes no difference whether 'you' are managing director or trainee manager. If letterwriting comes within your sphere, you need a collection of words and their meanings. The best is *The Shorter Oxford English Dictionary* – a witty title, as you will discover when you try to lift its two enormous volumes.

For everyday use, try something really short – but people's abilities is to be judged by the extent of their vocabulary and the precision with which they use it. So if you do not know the meaning of a word, or are doubtful as to its exact import, look it up.

Only a snob looks down on the illiterate, but lettered people (especially those who write letters for their living) invite derision if they mishandle words.

Those whose native tongue is not English have every excuse (see Chapter 31 – which includes some horrible examples). But for those born to speak English, it is vital that when their letters provoke laughter, they should do so by intention and not by mistake, that they should induce anger only by design; and that the words used should convey the intended meaning and have the desired impact.

To communicate accurately the meaning and intent of the writer is the object of a letter. Words are the weapons. Select yours with as much care as possible.

14

Clarity

It is a pity, then, that the average letterwriter can generally spare so little time for the drafting of missives. Naturally, draftsmen and lawyers use precedents, but even these precedents must be adapted. Words which were adequate for one situation may need careful alteration for another.

Suppose you write to prospective employees telling them that you will provide them with houses. Are they then entitled to refuse flats or bungalows? You should have written 'residences' or 'living accommodation' or 'homes'.

Do your assistants have restraint clauses in their contracts of service (see Chapter 63)? Do you describe with insufficient clarity the nature of the business which they are forbidden to follow when they leave you? Then the entire clause may be too vague to be enforceable.

You can probably find much better examples from your own disputes. Careful, precise use of the English language may take time in the short run but will eventually pay. Doubt destroys clarity; accurate wording eliminates doubt.

If you arrange for a builder to do work on your property but do not fix a price, a court would infer that you should pay a reasonable price. 'Obviously,' a judge would say, 'the parties must have intended that the contractors be paid for their efforts ... the inclusion of this clause was essential, to give the contract business efficacy.' In general, though, if the parties have not seen fit to provide for a situation, the courts will not do so for them. It is for you alone to make your deals.

Or suppose that you launch into freelance journalism. You agree to provide a feature for a trade paper. You should stipulate: 'If the article is returned to me within four weeks, then I shall accept it back without question. But if you keep it longer, it becomes yours.' This prevents any subsequent argument about the piece being sent 'on spec'.

The clearer your own thoughts, the better you will put them down on paper. The greater the clarity with which you write, the more likely it is that your writing will bring the results you seek. Unless you are deliberately trying to kick up dust so as to obscure some unpleasant issue, remember: unless your words are clear, they will not produce the effect you want.

15
Clichés & Clitches

Good business demands modern merchandising. Poor, primitive or commonplace packaging or publicity spells death for the product. Good merchandise may be wasted on the market thanks to bad presentation. 'Trite,' you say. 'You preach to the converted.'

'Trite, maybe,' I answer. 'But you have yourself answered with a cliché – which proves my point.' The same business people who accept that merchandising material, packaging and presentation must be original, striking, vital and vivacious are still prepared to package their own thought in words so well chewed that they nauseate.

Your thoughts, like your products, should be presented in bright, original wording. Impossible? Then at least avoid the aggravating cliché which slips so easily off the tongue but reveals lack of thought. 'The worse your case, the louder you should shout it,' proclaims the demagogue. Certainly the more unoriginal the thought, the more important is its disguise.

Have you ever listened to skilled politicians keeping their audience spellbound with words full of sound and fury but signifying nothing? Or sales people with a superlative spiel, wrapping their lines in clouds of persuasion to sell their goods hot, before their audience cools off.

How much more carefully, then, must writers mind their words and phrases. You want your correspondents to read your letters and to act on them? You would like them to provoke thought or sales or at least an appropriate and helpful reply? Then do the recipient the courtesy of avoiding the cliché.

Wit and humour help (see Chapter 17). So do quotations. Ordinary, short, simple, Anglo-Saxon words will do as well (see Chapter 13).

Rule 1: Never use a long word where a short one will do. Verbosity impresses only the writer.

Rule 2: The more important your message, the fresher the words should appear.

Below are some of my most hated clichés (or 'Clitches', as Ernest Bevin used to call them).

'In this day and age.'
'At this moment in time.'
'This is an historic and unique occasion.'
'This is a once only, unrepeatable and absolutely magnificent bargain offer.'
'The tip of the iceberg.'
'The buy of the year.'
'We must give of our best.'
'Each and every one of us must stand up and be counted.'
'We are moving full speed ahead.'
'Finally, and in conclusion.'

And beware of 'Quite frankly ... frankly speaking ... to tell you the truth ... honestly ... I'll be frank with you ... genuinely ... sincerely speaking ...' They may be only turns of phrase, but they do suggest that the writer is well capable of not telling the truth. Really honest and frank people do not need to hang notices round necks to tell the world of their integrity.

'We have the honour to be ... We beg to remain ... Your speedy response will oblige...' Ugh!

Clitches, ancient or modern, are a menace. When you are next bored at a meeting, make your own list. 'Much water will flow under the bridge ... many bridges to be crossed ...' How time will fly by.

And take as a dreadful warning Churchill's description of Anthony Eden's speeches as consisting 'entirely of clichés – clichés old and new – everything from "God is love" to "Please adjust your dress before leaving".'

As Samuel Goldwyn so expertly misput it: 'For heaven's sake let's have some new clichés!'

16
Officialese and jargon

For years I corresponded with a company secretary. 'Dear Sir,' he invariably began. 'Yours faithfully,' he ended. They were courteous but curt, and slightly overpowering in their aloof dignity. Obviously, I thought, the writer is a tough, remote man with whom it would be a great mistake to tangle.

I recently visited the company office for the first time. There I met the secretary – elderly, benign and gentle. He used his style of writing to disguise his personality and to keep his problems at bay. As he is an official, his letters reflect the policy of the board and the views of his superiors.

Official style, then, may provide a convenient shield; but official writers should still keep their words clear. There is no excuse for blunting meaning with useless jargon or clichés (see Chapter 15).

Even if a letter is routine, it should still be crisply worded, with a clear message.

Some of the most horrible examples of officialese are to be found in epistles from government departments or local authorities. Others emanate from bureaucrats of the commercial world.

'Vagueness may be necessary,' you say, 'to avoid making a decision, or to indicate that one has not been made. Clarity sometimes means unkindness while vagueness may cloak the unpleasant present with future hope.'

What does it mean? No one is saying that you must be tactless or cruel, but it is seldom kind to maroon the recipient of your letter in a sea of uncertainty, swelled by a flood of long, boring and mainly meaningless verbiage. Whether you write officially or unofficially, personally or impersonally, brevity and clarity should be the hallmarks of your style.

Use good precedents, where you can. Take your own drafts and rid them ruthlessly of every useless word, every ghastly jargon-ridden sentence. Shake off the padding and your bills for stationery, word processing or typing will shrink. A well-chosen word at the right time saves at least nine out of season.

Jargon may have its place as a cloak for the writer, but it should never be used to muffle meaning, or to obscure the daylight in the writer's thoughts.

17
Wit and humour

The humble pun has a bad name. Call it a play on words and it leaps back into fashion. Describe it as a *jeu de mots* and it is *à la mode* indeed.

Much of the best humour results from deft handling of the language. That is why jokes in foreign tongues are often so hard to enjoy.

Comedians or amusing speakers have many weapons at their disposal. Their art is part visual, part aural. The expression on their faces may matter as much as that which they give to their words. But writers depend on words alone. You may find this an advantage. There are no distractions. But still...

Novelists or fiction writers have the space to build up to comic situations. Even non–fiction writers have their humorous moments, using jokes or witticisms to point up morals or simply to enliven their style.

Letterwriters have less scope for humour and fewer words to play with. Their aim must be all the more sure. Puns have their place.

'You may bet your bottom dollar–if you will pardon the expression– that you will get more for your money with us.'

'This new line in pens will make its mark (in both senses of the phrase).'

'We were thinking of advertising these cut-price loos for customers who were none too flush– but persih the thought!'

Quick wit? Certainly not. A break, though, from the customary and boring. Even if the recipients groan at a pun, they may still wish they had perpetrated it themselves.

Irony and sarcasm

Sarcasm is supposed to be the lowest form of wit. Never mind. It has its moments. But it is designed to hurt: as there should never be hurt without design, use this form of attack with care.

Irony is sarcasm with the sting removed. You place your tongue firmly in your cheek, smile gently and (with luck) produce a chuckle from your reader.

'I know that you are immensely busy and incredibly overworked', you write to a representative who is reputed to have done nothing of late save sit on his rear axle or on that of the company car. 'But do you think that you could possibly spare the time to sell some of our new lines? If so, we should be much obliged. If not, then I trust that you will not think it unreasonable of us if we terminate your appointment.' You have to be precise. 'Just one month more within which to reach your target...' If that does not stir him into extracting his digit, nothing will. It is sarcasm, and justified.

Irony is more gentle. For instance:

'No doubt there are many reasons for your poor sales record. When you say it could be worse, perhaps you are right. But we would require some proof of that proposition. Meanwhile, could you suggest how we can survive the summer?'

At the expense of others

'Taking the mickey' is a pastime to be enjoyed with care. Those who tease the most may enjoy it least when fun is poked at themselves.

Not all of us are 'good sports' when the joke is on us. There is a vast difference between the private laugh in a confidential note and the same witticism in a letter which may be seen by others. In the first case, the recipient may join in the laughter. The second may cause humiliation and upset.

Voluntary self-mockery is different from being locked into the stocks in the village green. So assess the occasion carefully before you provoke laughter which may turn into ill-humour, ill-will—and lost profits or friends.

Make jokes at your own expense. The cost may be easier to bear.

The sting in the tail

A sting in the tail is the joy of all professional humourists. They lead you up one path, and then, when you think that you are in sight of the end, change direction so abruptly that you are left standing.

For speakers, as for tacticians, the element of surprise is vital. So is it also for writers of stories of suspense, detection or murder. It is a pity that it is not more often used by letterwriters seeking a dramatic and immediate effect. Some surprising examples:

Dear John,

Over the course of the past five years, you have earned my friendship and appreciation by a long series of considerable kindnesses. Today presents a memorable occasion. I have the biggest favour yet to ask of you!

Dear Mr Jones,

I fully appreciate that the defects in the machinery which we sold to you led to some considerable unpleasantness between us, all of which was our fault– or, to be completely accurate, that of this machinery which we imported from France. If you were to tear up this letter, you would have every justification in doing so, particularly as I am about to ask a favour of you. Will you be kind enough to allow us to replace the defective machine, at absolutely no cost to yourselves, with another of a different manufacture, for which we are now the agents? Our good name and goodwill are vital to us and...

Dear Joan,

I am writing to confirm that the time has come for your promised increase in salary. You have done a magnificent job and have earned the congratulations and appreciation of us all. The chairman, in particular, has asked me to say how greatly your services are valued.

However, you may wish to treat this letter as repudiation of your contract of service. As you know, the company is going through a period of very great financial crisis. So you and I are both being asked to accept a postponement of any increase in our salaries. I have accepted the situation. Will you?

Please would you come and see me? I have found this letter a very difficult one to write and would be immensely sorry to lose you as a colleague. As you know, we have great confidence in the future of the business. But the present is hell!

There are thousands of variations on this theme of the unexpected. Sometimes the twist is good for a laugh. Sometimes it is an introduction to an unpleasant shock. Sometimes there is only one gentle twist. Sometimes the letterwriter's path is full of hairpin bends. The reader's attention remains riveted to the writer's words. What's coming next?

Assuming that the writer is tactful, this off-beat approach will be appreciated. 'It's a miserable situation, but the man has a sense of humour...'; 'She is in a hell of a mess, isn't she? Still, things can't be too bad – at least she hasn't lost her sense of humour...'; 'At least life is never boring when you do business with him...' A tribute every time.

As always, judge the situation with care. Laughter and tears are close partners. A surprise that provokes a smile from one person may produce anger in another.

18

Similes and metaphors
– mixed and otherwise

Comparisons may be odious, but they provide a useful tool for the letterwriter. Use the word 'like' or 'as' and you have a simile.
Like:

> 'Our products are small and comparatively inexpensive but as essential as jewels in a fine watch.'
> 'Like jewels in a royal crown...'
> 'As welcome as the story's ending.'

Metaphors omit the 'like' or 'as'. For instance:

> 'We will hit them for six.'
> 'Our first ball.'
> 'Centre stump.'
> 'For a duck.'
> 'We fell at the first fence.'
> 'This time we've backed a winner.'

The vital rule with metaphors is not to mix them. Mix your drinks and you become sick. Mix your metaphors and your letter becomes ridiculous:

> 'If you want to hedge your bets, then try reversing the batting order and your scheme may turn up trumps.'
> 'Business is a battlefield in which poor players get skittled out, often at the first fence.'
> 'I'm sorry that we cannot give you more credit, but the banks are at our throat and squeezing us until the pips come out.'
> 'As the bishop said to the actress: "It's an ill wind that blows no one any profits, when it comes to reducing demand by putting the handcuffs on embattled industry".'

In a nutshell, good letters and mixed metaphors are as compatible as chalk and Chinese chopsticks, if you see what I mean.

Part 3

TACT AND TACTICS

'The last person we want to employ is a 'Yes-man' – don't you agree?'

19

Modesty matters

Royalty and editors use the word 'we'. By using the first person, writers retain their personality and avoid the impersonal and soulless approach. By avoiding the singular they add strength to their purpose. Without saying so, they indicate that their views are shared by others: ...colleagues, the company, public opinion, the nation....

There are two alternatives. The first is used by the French, the word *on* – 'one'. In English it is pompous and archaic. ' One does, does one?

'One knows your difficulties, but one must take into account the current shortage of credit...' One must indeed.

No, this will not do. 'One' is not pleased to accept your invitation to address the board – you are!

'We appreciate...' would be fine if you are writing on behalf of the board. 'We have checked our note of the conversation with you...' is plain silly if you are discussing your own conversation. 'We shall be pleased to come' is appropriate if you are bringing your spouse or friend, but if the acceptance is for yourself alone (assuming that you are not an extremely royal personage), the use of 'we' indicates either delusions of grandeur or a split personality, neither of which is likely to be appreciated by your hosts.

Some trades and professions have special usages. A one-man firm of solicitors may use the grand style, 'W...& Co.', and the accountant may acknowledge: 'We are in receipt of your letter.'

Equally, if you are replying to a letter received on behalf of the company or firm, it is correct to answer: 'We thank you for your letter dated the 14th...'. The thanks are those of the institution you represent and not yours personally. But if the letter came in an envelope addressed to you personally, and possibly marked 'Private and confidential' (for the legal rules, see Chapter 57), then you could almost certainly reply: 'I am grateful to you for writing to me...,' or 'I received your letter and will pass on your message to the board...'

When you are addressed as an individual and written to on a personal level, stick to the singular. When you write on behalf of the business, the plural is generally more apt, more modest and implies greater strength behind your pen.

What, then, of the contents of the letter? How far in a letter should you avoid the vertical pronoun: I?

Public speakers must beware of the immodest, boring, self-satisfied impression conveyed by smug use of the first person singular. 'I came; I saw; I conquered', said Julius Caesar. But he was a dictator and could get away with it. 'We came; we inspected; we took over', is far more appropriate to the modern business world. If you came on your own and can honestly say that you in turn were conquered by the excellence of the hospitality received, then that would be different.

'I am very grateful to you for making my visit so interesting...for sparing me so much of your time...for the trust you placed in me...' You speak personally and sincerely. You write on your own behalf, to thank the recipient for kindness accorded to you.

You may also wish to poke fun at yourself. It is safer than getting laughs out of the foibles of others. The inimitable Lord Denning delighted in saying,'When I used to sit and hear cases on my own, I could be sure that justice was done in my court. Now that I sit in the Court of Appeal, as one of a bench of three, the odds against justice being done are two to one.'

He can get away with it because he is man who combines extreme individuality and independence of mind with quiet and kindly courtesy. No one takes his jest seriously – least of all himself.

Writers who obviously see themselves as sitting either upon the throne of God, or at His right hand, are fools. If you have delusions of grandeur, then you would be wise to keep them to yourself or you may find yourself certified.

It is no excuse to protest, 'I am covering up for my inferiority complex'. Your correspondent may come to the same conclusion as the apocryphal psychiatrist – that you are just inferior!

It is not for you to shout aloud that you are great. One day you will descend, if only into retirement or the grave. Provoke jealousy by your words and you invite others to shake the tree – or even to pull it out by the roots. There is no need to go to the lengths of Uriah Heep: 'We are so very 'umble'. No one will believe you. Just write with humility, when you can. Modesty matters. Avoid that vertical pronoun and substitute the three letter word 'you'. It is the most important word in the language of communication. Take care not to fall into the trap in which Edith Sitwell found herself: 'I have often wished that I had time to cultivate modesty...but I am too busy thinking about myself.'

20

Flattery – and the great You Are

King Canute was overcome by the waves of false adulation. This sort of foolishness is as prevalent amongst commoners. It is stupid to emphasize 'the great I am' (Chapter 19), but the letterwriter should cash in on recipients' inevitably high regard for themselves. 'Love yourself,' said Oscar Wilde, 'and you are in for a lifetime of romance.' Business people are as romantic as all others.

The courtiers of Canute were intelligent people. The king did not suspect that he was being served a diet of lies. We all like to think the best of ourselves, so you cannot altogether blame the poor man. So use the courtiers' tactics.

Note, first, that flattery is as useful when your fight is up hill or when you are faced with an unpleasant opponent as it is when you are dealing with someone you admire. For instance:

'I have admired your work for so long that I would hate to fall out with you now...'
'You are a man most respected in this industry. So it really does grieve me to have to complain that...'
'I fully appreciate your integrity and good intentions but...'
'I cannot believe that a man of your high standing would write as you have done, had he known the facts...'
'I am sure that a company of the importance of yours would not willingly risk sacrificing its good name for the sake of...'

You must not underestimate your opposition. The essence of all sound flattery is apparent sincerity. People try to believe well of themselves, and if you share their admiration for their achievements you already have much in common. The higher and more powerful the executive, the more likely he or she is to be surrounded by adulators.

Still, where people achieve eminence in commerce you may expect them to be sound in judgement. Unless their power has corrupted them, they will be suspicious of the flatterer. So use subtlety to succeed.

Overdo your flattery and it sounds perilously close to sarcasm. 'Of course you know best...'; 'You are as wise as the three kings...'; 'Naturally, I would not think of arguing with you...'. Disastrous statements – and dangerous.

Here, then, are some useful examples of fine flattery, for use and adaptation to commercial occasions.

'Experience has taught me to value your views. It is therefore with great diffidence that I suggest that on this occasion you are wrong....'

'As you know, I rarely question your judgement – but have you considered...?'

'I am extremely grateful for the trouble you took in writing to me. I know how very busy you are and your courtesy is immensely appreciated. I do apologise, therefore, for having to take issue with you on just one or two points.'

'As you know, it is rare for me to take issue with you. I am very much a new boy in this business and rely greatly upon the advice and guidance of good friends, such as yourself. But...'

'I do appreciate your letter and I am sorry if I have caused offence where none was intended.

I am sure that you will appreciate the difficulty of my position. I am not a free agent. I have to follow the instructions of my board...'

'As usual, you are right. But dare I suggest...?'

'It is very rarely that you are wrong. But with great hesitation and after much research, I have come to the conclusion this time that...'

'We are old friends and you know the high regard that I have for you. Our understanding over the years has been built on frankness and I hope that you will not misunderstand my motives nor regard this letter in any way as an attack on your judgement nor, still less, as a slur on your integrity...'

'You are a marvel! I followed your suggestion which achieved precisely the desired results. Thank you very much. Now for the future. Perhaps we can cooperate on...'

21

The art of rudeness

A 'gentleman', or a 'lady', is never unintentionally rude. Intentional rudeness must be for some sensible purpose and designed for effect. In the theatre, it is taken for granted that an effect must be planned, created and perfected. In correspondence, planning equals preparation, precedent and thought. The effects which *require* the maximum of all three generally *receive* the minimum, because of anger or anxiety, hostility, dismay or urgency.

Attack usually produces that satisfying counterblast which relieves the writer's tension. You speak your mind so as to get your anger off your chest. 'I must get it out of my system' you say, or, 'Let's have it out ... I am not going to bottle it up...'

The metaphors are apt. Just as the penitent relieves a guilty conscience by frankness in the confessional, and your friends feel so very much better after pouring out their troubles into your sympathetic ear, so hostility is released through expression. Take it out of your mind and you may release it from your memory. 'I'm a frank person,' you say. 'I don't believe in false pretences. Much better to have it out.' (There we go again.)

All this is psychologically and physiologically sound, but it spells potential commercial disaster. If you get overheated and are unable to apply a thoughtful, careful mind to unpleasant personal situations, then a moment's misery may turn into permanent disaster. Your rude letter may result in loss and litigation, aggravation and upset – an exercise that is profitless in every sense of the word.

So the first rule on writing rude letters may generally be summed up in one word – don't. If the situation requires straight talking, then arrange to meet the other person and talk. By the time of the meeting you will have cooled down and your anger may have turned to understanding, your wrath to forbearance, and your probable loss of friends and profits to potential future business. You will also have preserved your good name and your reputation as a person of dignity and restraint. At worst, if you do let fly, then at least your loss of self-possession will not be recorded on paper.

'Sorry,' you say. 'We have been patient for long enough. We keep getting impertinent letters, and they require replies. I cannot allow foul-mouthed rudeness to my staff without some sort of vigorous response.' Or: 'I am sure that if I let off a real blast of indignation, I will bring them up short. Only rudeness will make them understand the seriousness of the position. A loud shout now may bring results.' Very well. Then sit back, consider and draft your words with care.

First, avoid foul language. You can be far more abusive with carefully considered, common words than with the four letter variety. So choose good words, with care. Remember the purpose for which they are intended and fire them with precise aim. Hone the razor's edge of your displeasure with the whetstone of your wit.

The turning of the cheek may be hard, but commercially it is generally sound. An angry word provokes like response. The writer who sounds off on paper through lack of self-control may regret his or her words when it is too late.

The right words in the right order stand a good chance of producing right results. But do use them with care. As Adlai Stevenson said, 'Man does not live by words alone, despite the fact that sometimes he has to eat them.'

In case you must be rude, here are some examples for your consideration.

Rebuttal of persistent allegations

Yes, we have received your letters containing the same allegations. We replied to the first half-dozen, but no useful purpose would be served by our answering each one. Unlike the wine which you and I used to enjoy together before you saw fit to end our friendship, your allegations do not mellow or improve with age.

I have long restrained myself from expressing my thoughts. But may we now regard this unpleasant correspondence as at an end?

Riposte to rudeness

Having allowed several days to pass since receiving your impertinent letter, I still regard your sentiments as the most unpleasant that I have seen on paper for a very long time. In the circumstances, unless you see fit to acquire some unaccustomed humility and to apologise, this correspondence – together with our business and personal relationships – is permanently at an end.

Note The absence of a sign-off (Yours faithfully) is extremely offensive. Silence is sometimes a good deal more expressive and useful than words. Hence the best answer to many unpleasant letters is simply to put them on file, without reply.

Brevity – the soul of brusqueness

This correspondence is at an end.

Sarcasm – to a (former) friend

Will you oblige me and go to hell? When you arrive, you will certainly find yourself in congenial company. I wish you a safe journey.

Brief end to long friendship

Will we pay you more, you ask? No – a thousand times. But not again in writing. My regard for you is no longer worth even a postage stamp.

So we'll sue

Maybe when you come before a court you will learn courtesy. We propose to provide you with the opportunity as swiftly as possible. Your rudeness is intolerable. This correspondence will now cease. Instead, we have instructed our solicitors to issue proceedings against you forthwith.

Two-letter word

No.

Throwing their words back in their teeth

We append a schedule containing particulars of the speeches, impertinent exclamations and expressions of rudeness which have finally suceeded in destroying, utterly and permanently, our regard for you and our business with you. If you were decent people we would expect a full apology. As it is, no doubt we shall hear nothing more from you. In one way, that will be a merciful relief.

Insensitivity incarnate

You are undoubtedly the closest approach to a rhinoceros ever to walk on two legs. If my poisoned darts have not yet penetrated your thick skin, then there is no hope for you. I can suggest that a holiday might help – and for all our sakes I would recommend a very long one, as far away from us as possible.

If you should return to town in recognizable human form, do please contact me. I shall be pleased to attempt to re-establish our relationship. You never know, we might be willing to place further orders with you. Do take care of yourself. There must be those who would miss you if you drove yourself to a premature grave.

Gloating over misfortune

Having received your letters– none of which, we thought, contained sufficient substance to merit a reply – we were not at all surprised to read of the judgement against you in the High Court last week. A few more like that and no doubt your company will be wound up. In that happy event, would you be kind enough to let us know, so that we may have the pleasure of attending the creditors' meeting?

Water off a sheep's back

As the PR people say, 'There is no substitute for wool'. If proof of this were required, your letter would serve admirably. It has no other apparent purpose.

The really effectively rude letters are usually those in which the words are barbed with wit or sarcasm, but which have an outward appearance of charm. The most devastating rudeness in speech is generally perpetrated with a sweet smile on the face.

To lose your temper is a sign of defeat. To lose it in court is often to lose your case. To lose it on paper is always to lose face and forfeit the full effect that your words could otherwise have.

So keep cool, won't you? And address your letters with care, marking the envelopes (where appropriate) 'Personal and confidential'. Watch out for libel (Chapter 52), but rejoice that it is not defamatory to tell people to their faces precisely what you think of them. But when you dictate a letter, your secretary (at least) will know its contents. So there will have been 'publication', and if your words are defamatory you could be at risk.

22

Rude retorts – at leisure

'How I wish I'd thought of that,' we all say, half an hour after we have made a lame reply to a rude remark. The devastating riposte, the unanswerable counter-thrust, the really rude retort salted with a touch of wit – these so seldom come to mind when you want them.

Replies to rudeness – in kind but with compound interest – are much easier when the initial attack was made by letter. So now suppose that your other cheek has been turned so often that it is sore, that you are determined to lash out at last. Then remember that there can be no general rule as to the best words for the occasion. You must match your wit to the words of your opponent. You must parry thrusts at the point of impact and hit back where it hurts most.

Here are a few sample suggestions:

We suggest that the best way for you to appreciate the poverty of your case would be for you to read the words with which you have seen fit to clothe it. We are not referring to the grammatical or typing errors when we say that those words are as incomprehensible as they are discourteous.

The emptiness of your threats is equalled only by the poverty of your product.

By resorting to blatant incivility you have not lowered the level of your case. It started below ground. May we respectfully suggest that you let it rest in peace? If you see fit to disinter it again, we shall have it cremated by our lawyers.

We are not at all surprised that you have descended to common abuse. A dried pea always rattles loudest.

How kind of you to reveal yourself so admirably on paper. Your charming words are appreciated for what they are – a smoke screen.

We are, of course, sorely tempted to tell you to go straight to hell. But as this is an experience which you will doubtless have already had and enjoyed, no useful purpose would be served thereby. Instead, we recommend that you strive desperately for the other place. Were you to change your ways completely, you never know your luck. Meanwhile, we do not intend to allow you to make our business life into a purgatory.

If we were to descend to your level of abuse, our words would acquire the same odium as already attaches to yours. Suffice it, then, to say ...

If you manufactured fine sticks and stones, instead of cloth or ships, or shoes, or sealing wax, as the case may be then your words might break our bones. As it is, we suggest that you re-read them. They provide a really excellent mirror, revealing the writer's mind ...

And your guide to replies:
1. Never descend to common abuse (it is too common to be effective).
2. Never lose your cool. In person, this may be difficult; on paper the heat of the moment can always be allowed to pass – there is no excuse for breaking this rule.
3. Bland discourtesy is best: the rude retort hidden in the sting of an apparently polite remark.
4. There is no better way to annoy your opponents than to laugh at them; apparently gentle words may have far greater effect than any vulgar obscenity.

There is, of course, one grave disadvantage to launching a written counter-attack. You will not be there when your letter is opened, so you will not be able to observe the effect it has on the enemy. Now, if you hear no more about the claim which your opponents were intending to make upon you, or if in contrast to your quiet, balanced and witty words, the crudity of their attacks becomes apparent – then you will probably have won.

23

Warning, complaining, and tearing off strips

The heat of the moment produces steam which should not be let off till you have cooled down. If you must explode, then do so out loud and resist the temptation to put your feelings into writing: 'least said, soonest mended'.

You may need to express your wrath on paper for the record – for instance, to prove why you rejected a product or dismissed an employee. Alternatively, you may prefer to write because you can choose your words with greater care, so that if they are used against you, you are less likely to regret them. Or you may wish the recipient to consider your views at leisure.

You must take particular care to match your words, which must always be calm, to the precise nature of the occasion (see also Chapter 24 on turning the other cheek and Chapter 22 on retorts to rudeness). Some useful examples:

> We enclose herewith a schedule, setting out in detail the assurances you have given and broken in recent months. How much longer do you expect us to endure this sort of treatment?

> We have not completely given up hope of an improvement in our treatment at your hands, but we are about to do so.

> Our patience is exhausted. This must be your last chance.

> Please do not ignore this letter as you have seen fit to ignore those of .... Next time we shall not write, but take action.

Commercial correspondence is full of dread warnings of dire results. Some are gentle, some cruelly outspoken, some kind, some cruel. Here are some examples, to be threaded appropriately into your admonitory letter:

> We have had to complain many times in the past concerning .... If we have cause to repeat our complaints in the future, then inevitably...

We realize that this is the first complaint concerning your ... But you must appreciate that this is a matter of grave concern to us. We must warn you that if there is any repetition, then ...

I shall not warn you again ...

Please accept this warning in place of the action which we would have to take if there is any repetition in the future ...

The partnership between warnings and complaints is by now sadly obvious. Either may be fended off with the appropriate action, or often by an apology (see Chapter 25). The art of complaining is itself worth careful study and is not always allied to a warning. Before you rattle your sabre, you must ensure that your adversary will be suitably impressed. If not, then threats and warnings are out, but you can still complain.

Complaints, then, may sometimes be allied with threats or warnings, but are often quite as effective on their own. Indeed, where a threat would be laughable or provocative it is in any event better left out.

The complainant's first task is to discover the best ear in which to pour his poison. Do you go straight to the top person, knowing that as a result you will antagonise the junior person with whom you have dealt? Or do you exercise patience and keep your complaints on a lower level? Do you let off commercial steam to your trade association or Chamber of Commerce, or try your luck with your adversary's trade or professional association? Only experience can tell. Only after thought should you decide.

The complaint itself may be incensed or outraged in tone, or more in sorrow than in anger. All depends on the results you seek. Here are a few useful lines:

We would be pleased to retain our association with you but ...
We are sure that you personally could have no idea of ...
We wish this were the first time that we had cause to complain about ...
We are very anxious to avoid embroiling the board in ... but ...
We are sorry to trouble you personally regarding the sins of your subordinates, but ...
We have so far restrained ourselves from complaining, but ...
We have complained many times. This is the last.

To be able to turn hostility into a friendship or a row into a firm, fat order – this is the mark of the skilful commercial letterwriter. Call it cynical if you like, but if through your calculated coolness you can make the other person feel like a worm, then you will avoid acquiring a needless enemy and you may exchange enmity for amity – with profit.

Turning the other cheek, then, may require self-control, but if you cannot control yourself, you should not be in charge of others.

Even after the outbreak of hostilities, all is not necessarily lost. 'Softly, softly catchee monkee', says the oriental sage. Cool customers are admired, hotheads lose custom.

So think carefully before you fire off any letter like those in the last chapters. Instead, re-read some of the flattering phrases in Chapter 20, and see if you cannot find the inspiration and the words to change your correspondent's wrath into gold.

24

In a tight corner

In times of trouble we often tend to draw analogies from the world of sport in general, and from fencing and boxing in particular: a cutting remark, a debating thrust, out for the count, hit below the belt, in a tight corner, and so on...

If you are in difficulties, you must choose your words with special care. In order to emerge unscathed, you have three alternative courses of action. You can throw in the towel, trade blow for blow, or duck smartly under your opponent's fist and skip nimbly away.

For a change, let's take our first example from the speaker's world. (See *Janner's Complete Speechmaker and Compendium of Retellable Tales*.)

You are proposing a toast to the bride and groom. The bride's father is dead. The groom's parents are divorced. What do you do?

You can surrender by making no mention of the parents. This is abject cowardice, and would be generally regarded as such.

You can neatly duck the situation with a few carefully chosen sentences: 'The bride's father ... We wish he were here not only in spirit ... but he would have been proud and happy today ... How pleased we are that our groom's parents are both so well – and here together, celebrating with us ...'

Finally, you can take the bull by the horns (to take an analogy from another sport). Starting with the sort of comment given above, you can extend it into the appropriate elegy and eulogy. 'Let us face it, ladies and gentlemen – no occasion is completely perfect, no life without its problems. How sad we are that the bride's father is not here ... but we admire her mother doubly for the fortitude with which she bore her loss and especially for the courageous and splendid way in which she brought up the bride .... The extent of her triumph is revealed by the radiance of our bride today.

'We know, too, that our groom's parents sit together with him, united in their joy at his happiness and good fortune ...'

Now suppose that you are writing to the family. You cannot attend their celebration. Normally, the less said about difficulties and differences, the better. 'With you in *our* happiness,' reads the cable from afar. 'How sad we are that we cannot join you,' goes the letter. But where the parties are close to you and you have to write at greater length, the above principles still apply. Hence:

> As you know, I was an old friend of your father. I know how delighted he would have been at your choice of bride.
>
> I am writing to you both, although I know that you are now apart – you will, I am sure, be together for the great day. How I wish I could make up a trio. I admire so much the way in which, despite your differences, you have always managed to be so understanding when it came to relationships with your son. You must be proud of him.

There are plenty of equivalent situations in business. The surrender is achieved by an apology (see Chapter 25). The counterattack is explained in Chapter 22 (on retorts to rudeness). The form of ducking away from trouble to be adopted will (as always) depend upon the circumstances. Here are some useful opening gambits:

> We fully appreciate the circumstances which have led to the anger and disappointment expressed in your letter. There is another side to the story and we do hope that you will give it your earnest consideration.
>
> You are right – but...
>
> I do see your point of view – but am sure that you will give consideration to mine ...
>
> Yes, we made a mistake – but in all good faith. The situation nevertheless remains that ...
>
> We see your viewpoint. Now please do consider ours.
>
> Your letter admirably sets out your case. It is only courteous, then, for us to set out as fully as possible the situation as we see it ...
>
> Thank you so much for your promptness in dealing with our complaint. We appreciate your letter – and your viewpoint. We hope that, on reflection, you will agree that ...
>
> No, we do not agree with you. But nevertheless ...

Those who use words as weapons employ very similar tactics to those of the fencer or boxer. You give way a little, so as to attack a lot. You retreat gently, so as to counter-attack with firmness. You at least pretend to see the other person's viewpoint so that he or she will be prepared to consider yours. Alternatively, you politely disagree – and then show your magnanimity and/or good sense or goodwill by then offering a compromise on some point, however small.

The French put it well: '*Il faut reculer pour mieux sauter*' – you must withdraw, the better to leap forward.

There are occasions, of course, when you have your back to the wall, there is no room for retreat, all escape routes are cut off, you are up against the ropes...Then remember the advice given to police officers: 'Tuck yourself neatly into the corner and use your fists, your knees, your truncheon ... At least if you are in that corner, they will not be able to get a knife in your back ...' Unless, of course, they knock you unconscious and drag you out.

When desperate, try these gambits:

> If you see fit to make these allegations to third parties, we shall have no hesitation in putting the matter in the hands of our solicitors.
>
> Your threats are as empty as the premise upon which you base your allegations is groundless. Nevertheless, if you wish to take the matter further, we must refer you to our solicitors.
>
> We regard your allegations as both impertinent and groundless. If they are repeated, we shall take such steps as our lawyers advise, to protect both our position and our good name.
>
> If you are so ill-advised as to carry out your threats, then kindly direct all further correspondence to our solicitors.
>
> In one, last, desperate attempt to remedy a situation which (we repeat) is not of our making, our Mr Jones will contact you and try to arrange some convenient time to visit your office.
>
> Our chairman will be in touch with yours.

In the last resort, then, you have three alternatives. First, you can pass your correspondence to your lawyers, possibly in the hope that if you put on a sufficiently bold legal front your enemies will stay in their own trenches. You can cast aside pride or convention and try the personal approach, at whatever level seems best. Or you can remain silent.

An aged employee used to keep a little wooden sign hanging on the wall by her desk: 'Silence is golden', it read. On occasion – indeed, on more occasions than most people realize – the adage is a good one.

One way to emerge unscathed from a tight corner is to cover your face with your arms, crouch low, and pray for the sound of the bell.

25

Apologies

One of the most valuable words in the English language is 'sorry'. If you are liable to lose your shirt, try displaying a white sheet. The effect on your adversaries can be quite startling. When people get what they want, when their pride is satisfied by the humbling of their opponent, they are willing to forgive a very great deal. So every skilled letterwriter must know how to wield a dignified apology.

In the commercial world even apologies must be driven home with due care. If you have admitted fault or liability on paper – even by implication – you will be in trouble if you afterwards try to change your mind.

If you are involved in a road traffic accident, for instance, in which there is damage to person or property, an admission of liability may rob you of your insurance cover. Insurers do not wish to lose the chance to fight a case, if they see fit, through some premature genuflection by the insured.

Or take the common case of the supplier or contractor concerned to preserve the goodwill of a complaining customer.

The customer writes, moaning mightily. Instead of replying with a firm denial of liability and contradiction of the customer's allegations, the anxious supplier or contractor simply replies: 'I'm terribly sorry .... We greatly regret .... We shall do everything possible to put things right ...' The customer cannot be satisfied and refuses to pay the bill. The supplier or contractor sues.

'Look at the correspondence,' retorts the debtor. 'We put all our complaints into writing. They were never denied. On the contrary, the plaintiffs apologised and expressed their regrets. It's a weak excuse to say that they only did this to preserve our goodwill, isn't it?' Weak or not, it is one that is commonly heard in courts.

So take care before you assuage the customer or client who takes umbrage by apologising in writing. If you feel that your best position is prostrate, arrange an interview. Any apology in writing is more likely to be used in evidence against you – unless you mark it 'without prejudice'(see Chapter 61).

That said, the art of graceful apology is still worth careful study. Here are some common and helpful forms of apology, to be incorporated into your letters when it is necessary or advisable to do penance on paper.

> Despite our every effort, these errors occurred – and we do apologise. We trust that no substantial or lasting harm was done and we are pleased to have the opportunity to put things right.

> We apologise most sincerely for any apparent discourtesy. None was intended.

> We greatly regret that you were offended by .... We are sorry that you took offence when none was intended.

> While we are extremely sorry that you felt that ... we must nevertheless point out that ...

> We are always anxious to have satisfied customers and therefore we are prepared to assist by ....We are in any event sorry that you were dissatisfied but we must point out that in making this offer, we do so without prejudice to our contention that ... and no liability whatsoever is admitted.

> I am asked by our board to say how much it is regretted that .... The Directors trust that you will accept their assurance that ...

> We apologise most sincerely for ...

26

Lies – black and white

Some lies are forgivable. The letterwriter needs to know how best to disguise the truth.

Sometimes, the truth is just too horrible to tell. Imagine starting a letter: 'I finally decided to skip our lunch because I could not bear the thought of spending an hour in your company.' Or: 'The reason why our chairman refused to speak to you is that he regards you as an unmitigated crook.' Much better to say: 'Terribly sorry, but I must ask you to be kind enough to postpone our lunch. The chairman has decided to descend upon us that very day! Or: 'I do hope that you were not offended by any apparent discourtesy on X's part. Certainly none was intended.'

These of course, are examples of the white lie, designed by those without defence to avoid offence. When the truth would hurt or humiliate, even the moralist forgives the untruth.

What, then of the inexcusable whopper – the blatant lie, told for one's own good only? As courts of law are not courts of morals and justice is sometimes cruel, a book on the letterwriter's craft is no place for moral homilies. If lies must be told, though, at least tell them well. I suggest the following ten commandments for the purpose:

1 Check all previous correspondence and documents, to ensure that the truth is not apparent from your own previous writings.
2 Comb through your own recollection, and check with that of your colleagues, to ensure that nothing has already been said to your correspondents which would now nail you as a liar.
3 If you can avoid putting the untruth on to paper, then do so. The telephone is a useful instrument for the purpose, but remember: there may be a machine at the other end of the line recording your words; and while a contract made orally is as binding as any in

writing, its existence and its terms are far harder to prove (see Chapter 58).

4 If you do decide to use the telephone as an instrument of untruth, then *you* have the conversation taped, if you can. One lie is bad enough, but to compound it with a contradictory untruth next time is unforgivable. A record of your words will prevent this.

5 If you must record your lie on paper, then cash in on the ambiguities of the English language try to make your words as vague as possible and capable of at least two interpretations.

6 Prepare an escape route in case of need. Maybe the transposition of a comma would alter the meaning back to the truth, so that you could then say: 'I do apologise for the misunderstanding, which was entirely due to a clerical error.'

7 If found out and there is no apparent excuse, be prepared to write: 'Although the letter went out under my reference, it was in fact written by my former assistant, Mr Jones, during my absence. I would like to emphasize the word "former". As a result of this episode, he has been dismissed.'

8 It is always better to have your untruthful letters signed by someone else, even in your name. Thus: 'You will observe that the signature at the foot is in my name but not in my writing. This was an inexcusable liberty taken by my then assistant, Mr Jones. He has been dismissed as a result. Thank you for drawing this matter to our attention.' (The fact that there never was a Mr Jones is irrelevant.)

9 When you recieve a letter containing a lie, remember the above stratagems – they may be used against you; and study Chapter 27 for suitable ripostes.

10 Where the lie is a large one, you have two alternatives: you may either build up to it by a series of minor fibs, or you can shout the big fib from the start, in capital letters. Thus: 'I fear that you could not properly have read my previous letters to you, which state quite clearly that ...' Or: 'I had not wanted to tell you, but it is necessary now to make a completely clean breast of it. The fact is that ...' (The fact, of course, is fiction.)

Remember the eleventh commandment and keep it wholly. *Be not caught.*

You may, of course, take this chapter with as many pinches of salt as suits your literary palate. But like it or not, the lying letter is as much a fact of business and social life as the lying witness is a regular occupant of the witness-box. It may take one thief to catch another, but you do not need to be a liar to recognize one. Still, to appreciate the tricks of their trade you must know them. So if it makes you feel better, re-read this chapter from that viewpoint only. Then look at replies to lies.

27

Replies to lies

Call someone a liar and you make an enemy. Suggest that he is mistaken and he may well agree. If you receive a letter containing untruths – however plainly stated – pause and look, before you leap to retaliate in kind. Self-restraint pays dividends.

There are many ways of turning aside untruths from others. A touch of sophistry is definitely justified. Churchill (who was forbidden by the rules of parliamentary debate to denounce a colleague as a liar) referred to an untruth as 'a terminological inexactitude'. A lie by any other name ... More recently Cabinet Secretary Sir Robert Armstrong admitted in court that he had been 'economical with the truth'.

Here are some suggested ripostes to the lying letter:

I fear that whoever gave you the information upon which your letter is based is himself in error. *(The height of tact, this – your correspondent saves face from the start and is given every opportunity to withdraw without humiliation – an essential in commercial warfare as in any other.)*

I am sure that it is no fault of yours, but clearly your conclusions are founded on a misunderstanding of the facts.

I am most anxious that there should be no misunderstandings between us. If you would be kind enough to refer to our letter of ... you will see that the facts are not quite as you have stated.

I fear that our recollections of our conversation do not accord. I am quite sure that we agreed that ... I have confirmed this with our Mr Jones, who was present. *(What a pity that you did not confirm it in writing. Or maybe you did. Or if your letter is in response to one from him which purports to confirm the conversation but gets it wrong, then one up to you for actually reading his letter before you filed it. Beware of so-called letters of confirmation which are in fact travesties of the truth.*

I am sorry, Jane, but you are wrong. We have known each other long enough to speak frankly, without ill-will or rancour. I am sure that the cause of the trouble was the report of .... I know that under no circumstances would you have written as you did, had you appreciated that .... I fear that Mr Green must have led you astray.

All my fault, I am sure – obviously I have not made myself clear.

As I am sure your letter was not intended to be offensive, I shall reply in full ....

I wish I had followed your suggestion and got everything into writing. As it is, your letter suggests that unless we can get things cleared up fairly fast, we shall get involved in misunderstandings which neither of us wants. Why don't we meet for lunch?

I am sorry, but I simply cannot accept the allegations contained in your letter. These are founded on an obvious misunderstanding of the situation. Perhaps it would help if I outlined our views, in full.

These gambits are handy whether or not your correspondent has in fact been rude or offensive to you. After all, he may have told an untruth or misstated the situation with a smile on his pen (to mix our metaphors – Chapter 18). But there are times when rudeness is too blatant to be ignored. This does not mean that you should reply in kind. Here are some suggested gentle retorts:

We have done business together for many years and I still hope that we shall do so in the future – to our mutual advantage. In the circumstances, I shall not reply to your letter in like tone.

We have known each other for a long time and I really am shocked at the way in which you have seen fit to write. I think that someone is stirring the pot. The statements you make are untrue, but I am sure that these have arisen out of a misunderstanding, probably created by someone who hopes to drive us apart. Let us keep cool. I would be happy to meet you.

Surely it does not help the situation to write as you have done? In the circumstances, I shall resist the temptation to answer in like terms. It is a great pity that we are at loggerheads. This is, I am convinced, unnecessary. Let's try to make new start, shall we?

If I do not answer your rude letter with an even ruder one, I hope that you will not take this as a sign of weakness. Equally, it would not help if I were to indicate my views about the misstatements which turn your letter into fiction. I would prefer that we try to revert to where we were before this correspondence started, in the hope that we can clear up the mess without the entire matter landing in the hands of lawyers. If we are no longer to do business together, so be it. But at least let us be civilized. It may help if I set out the facts as I see them.

You may have noticed that in this sort of reply the cliché comes in handy. The set phrase helps conceal the unsettled temper. 'You are in error ... you are mistaken ... we regret that you are misinformed ...' – all much better than 'you are wrong', and almost invariably infinitely preferable to 'you are a damned liar' – even if that is the truth. As every merchandiser and PR person knows, both a product and its presentation need careful wrapping up. The noble art of the skilful wrap-up should form part of every course on commerce, with special reference to the reply to lies.

28

On a personal note

In general, personal notes should be written by hand. This is far more troublesome and time-consuming than dictating – which is one reason why the handwritten note is so appreciated. Whether you are sending congratulations or commiserations, apologies or thanks, three lines written are often better than three pages typed.

If you cannot spare the time to write (literally), then at least make sure that you 'top and tail'. Have the body of the letter word-processed, if you must, but write in 'Dear Joe' and 'yours sincerely, Martin.' Or at least add a handwritten PS.

Naturally, it is helpful if your writing can be read. If you are taking time to write, then at least spare the extra few moments to do so without the apparent haste which the erratic line and the smudged sentence so clearly indicate.

If you want a good reason for careful writing (courtesy apart), then remember that there are those who specialize in reading character from script. This may, of course, be a good reason for having your letters typed, but it also explains why many prospective employers, when advertising for staff, say 'Please send full details in your own handwriting'.

The object of a personal note is to convey personal thoughts. The more impersonal the form of the note typed (word-processed or, much worse, duplicated), the less its effect. Conversely, any personal touches are welcome.

The method of writing matters. So also does the method of delivery. For details of normal postal arrangements, please see Appendix 1; but if you can manage to send your missive by hand, marking the envelope accordingly, you are setting a special seal of importance, thought and urgency on the contents. Recipients also see that you have taken trouble.

Handwritten notes should generally be separate, however short they are, although there are times when they can be added to something else. If, for instance, you have to send a printed circular to a friend, then add a note at the foot in your own handwriting. Or perhaps invitations are going out for a company party. These have to be printed. Then add a few words at the bottom: 'Do come! – Johnny,' or 'I look forward to seeing you – Mary.'

Do you especially want the recipient to come to a meeting? Add a footnote: 'PLEASE be there – I need you!' or, 'A full turn-out is vital. I know you are terribly busy, but I would be immensely *grateful* if you could come.

Impersonal notes are destined for the fire or waste basket. The more personal the tone you adopt, the greater the impact. So be personal.

29

Letters overseas – customers and their customs

The traditional caricature of the Englishman? At home, polite but humourless, sitting silently in a train, talking to no one; abroad, a phlegmatic figure, waiting silently for a foreigner who speaks English. In fact this person will soon have followed the dodo into extinction. Nowadays, most English abroad will 'have a go' at the foreign language, even at the risk of making fools of themselves. They know that if they wish to make friends or to influence business in their direction, they must make the necessary effort.

Take Americans entering world markets. They will arrange crash courses covering not only the foreign languages needed but also local customs. They know that customers have customs which are to be respected.

Curiously, these rules, which are self-evident in courteous commercial conduct on the personal level, are often disregarded when people put pen to paper or (more likely) mouth to dictating machine.

Peruse almost any file of correspondence with a foreigner. The letters will be filled with jargon scarcely comprehensible even to the writer's compatriots. Jargon is bad enough on the home market (where it may do grave damage – see Chapter 16), but it can leave overseas customers in despair.

You may, of course, point with justification to painfully correct and cliché-ridden letters received from Germany, for instance, with verbs placed at the end of lengthy sentences and the writer having, as always, the honour to be your most obedient and respectful servant. To every nation its style, and if you wish to do business with them you must respect that style.

So what is the answer? There are two possibilities only. Either write your letters in the foreign language concerned, or use the English language in the way that is least alarming to foreigners.

Unless you are yourself expert in the nuances of the foreign tongue, my advice is to keep it for convivial speech or tabletalk, and not for business letters (except, perhaps, for friendly, non-commercial postscipts). There are enough misunderstandings in international affairs without your adding to them by mangling the language on paper. By all means flatter and please foreigners by conversing in their own language, but let your efforts stop there. If you employ an interpreter or translator make sure he or she is bilingual and totally trustworthy. Only those who are sensitive to shades of meaning in *both* languages can do the job properly. And to be on the safe side, send the English version together with the translation.

Truly bilingual people are rare. Some of the difficulties are obvious even when you consider the differences in idioms used by peoples who ostensibly all speak English. I once saw the end of an American romance when I assured my New York girl friend that I would 'knock her up at six'. Differences between lifts and elevators, braces and suspenders, pavements and sidewalks – all should be known. And please note: in the USA, rubbers are worn on the feet.

Or take pronunciation. The overseas lecturer who explained how the invading forces landed on the beaches and created peace for the inhabitants caused chaos by his charming pronunciation of the words 'beaches' and 'peace'. Letterwriters may at least rejoice that foreign words on paper do not have to be pronouned. But spelling may prove crucial.

When you do write in English, all the rules in Chapters 10 and 11 apply with even more force. The simpler the language the less likely it is that the recipient will misunderstand; the shorter the sentences and the clearer the thoughts, the better the business you are likely to do.

Like all rules, these have their exceptions. If you are trying to delay, then selective sentences of specially contrived jargon may send the foreign correspondent scuttling for his dictionary or (better still) off to join the queue at the local translators. He may even write back to seek elucidation.

If you doubt these suggestions, consider how much pleasanter and more profitable your dealings with your overseas correspondents would be if they treated you as you are advised to treat them. Not for nothing did the Tower of Babel collapse. Some sensible goodwill, simple phrases, trained translators – these might have kept the building erect to this day.

30

The human races

The recipients of your letters may be as prejudiced as you are, but they may not be so ready to recognise their defects. Alternatively, you may be dealing with someone of genuinely open and intelligent mind. So if you are tempted to salt your letters with remarks which might be interpreted as racist, or otherwise offensive, don't.

Take the Scots or the Irish for instance. They may delight in making jokes about avarice and whisky or brogue and the Blarney Stone (as the case may be), but this does not mean that they will like it when they come from others. The best raconteurs of anti-Semitic stories are Jewish. We are entitled to laugh at our own miseries and we recognize that it is our sense of humour, as much as any other quality, that has enabled us to survive. But no Jew appreciates an anti-Semitic joke coming from a non-Jew, even a close friend. Jokes about popes, pills and priests may go down splendidly in Protestant circles. But in a letter even a hint of anti-Catholic prejudice may spell ruin.

'We would never Welsh on you.' 'Like an Arab market place.' 'Eeny, meeny, miny, mo' – expunge them all. A reference to Eskimo Nell may be well received, but the popularity of the Harlot of Jerusalem is far from universal.

Normally, no civilized person wishes to cause unnecessary offence (for the correct use of rudeness, see Chapter 22). Avoid sexist jokes and references too: nowadays they are more likely to offend than amuse (and don't forget, that letter you started 'Dear Sir' is quite likely to land on a woman executive's desk). Even if you do not agree with the customs of your fellows, at least accord them respect.

There is an ancient rabbinical saying: 'Respect goes before the law'. Respect for the ways, feelings, attitudes and ideas of others is even more important than adhering to the letter of the law.

31

Following up and closing the deal

The matador hopes to kill his quarry with the first thrust of his sword. If he succeeds, he may be awarded one or both ears and (most exceptionally) the tail as well. The letterwriter may make a killing at the first blow − so earning profit, an appointment, a prize or some other happy result. But a follow-up may be vital, to clinch, to close, to succeed.

The following list of memory-joggers, adaptable to most occasions, may be helpful.

I did appreciate the time you gave to me. Could you spare, please, just a little more to answer my letters?

At the risk of becoming a bore, may I please remind you ...

I do know how very busy you are, and I would therefore doubly value a reply to ...

I do not seem to have received a reply to my letter of the ... I am quite sure that this is due to an oversight on your part, but your early attention would be greatly appreciated.

I would not dream of pressing you, were I not myself under pressure.

I fear that unless you can kindly make your decision shortly, I shall most reluctantly be forced to ...

I know that I have written to you before concerning ... I hope you will not mind my doing so once again.

I refer to my letters of the..., the...,the...and the....Could I now *please* have the courtesy of a reply?

I fear that unless I receive a reply to my letters within seven days, I shall have to....

I am sure that you intend no discourtesy by ignoring my letters, but on reflection you will agree I hope that it will not help us.

You frame your reminder to suit its purpose. If your first effort fails, do not be afraid to try again. The more trying you become, the more likely you are to succeed.

32

Introductions and references

The greatest favour that you can do for most people is to provide them with the right sort of introduction. 'What matters to good advocates is not to know their law,' said the wise old practitioner, 'but to know their judges.' In every field it is *whom* as much as *what* you know that matters. Match the introduction or reference to victim or recipient.

Letters of introduction and reference require special care. If they are inaccurate or negligent, you could be in trouble. If a reference is defamatory, then you could rely upon the defence of 'qualified privilege', but if 'malice' is alleged against you, it could be a long, hard fight. Nor is a disclaimer a defence against a negligence claim by your victim (see Chapter 56).

The best introductions and testimonials are the briefest. An excess of superlatives destroys the effect. I suggest:

To whom it may concern

I am pleased to recommend Mr James Blank, who has been employed as a ... in my department for ... years. I have found him reliable, diligent, cheerful and helpful. We are very sorry that he is leaving us.

I would be grateful for any assistance you could give to Mrs Mary Brown, who has supplied this company with ... over the course of ... years. We have now moved into a different line of production and can no longer make use of her products. However, we are happy to recommend her and them to you.

I am pleased to provide a reference for Mr William Jones. He is a man of energy, tact and initiative who is leaving us because we have been obliged to close down his department. We cannot offer him the prospects of promotion which he deserves. If you require any further information, please do not hesitate to contact me personally.

Finally, remember to disclaim, loudly and clearly, in all appropriate cases. If a reference or testimonial is given carelessly and causes damage to the recipient, it will be no answer for you to say that you were not paid for providing it (see Chapter 52).

Examples:

> Whilst we are pleased to assist by providing references/information/advice, these are given on the strict understanding that no legal liability of any sort is accepted in respect thereof, by the company, its servants or agents.

> The above reference/testimonial is given without legal responsibility.

> No responsibility can be accepted in respect of the above reference/testimonial.

My favourite reference is to be avoided:

> I am pleased to recommend Roger Green for any other job!

Part 4

LETTERS FOR OCCASIONS

'If we accept your claim for allowances, we owe you £30.'

33

Letters that sell

Whatever your business, you must sell. Whether you are a manufacturer, a wholesaler, a retailer, a stockist of services – whatever your trade, industry or profession ... the moment that you stop selling, your business starts dying.

Some goods or services sell themselves. Happy are they who can simply sit back and live off them. Sadly the vast majority of us must earn our daily bread through selling.

Some sales may be made face to face. The larger the item, the more profitable it becomes to devote personal time to seeing the potential customer. Customers may be bearded in their dens or addressed as part of an audience. Or direct sales may be made through advertisments (not the province of this book) or by direct mail (see Chapter 48). But a great number of the best sales are won through the right letters landing on the customer's desk, or are lost because those letters are off the mark.

There is no such special creature as the sales letter. Nearly every letter is trying to sell something. Maybe it is goods or services; your case for an overdraft or an indulgence; or simply your good name or goodwill.

It follows that if you seek a direct or indirect sale through the mail, all the normal rules in this book apply to your letter. For instance, you must pay proper attention to the envelope (Chapter 44) and stationery (Chapter 43); to the presentation of the contents and in particular to the methods of reproduction (Part 6). Your message must be concise (Chapter 12) – 'Brevity is the soul of sales', as one top merchandising man puts it. You must consider ways of signing on and off (Chapter 2) and pay careful heed to opening and closing with a punch (Chapter 1). You should use flattery (Chapter 20), humour (Chapter 17) and sound and sensible modern grammar (Chapters 10 and 11).

There are some special problems. After a careful study of your market and bearing in mind the limitations of letterwriting, what is your best approach to the sale of your particular goods or services?

If you have your prospects sitting across the lunch table, if you have 'found them at their desks', if you are chatting them up in your shop or showroom, or at your stand at a trade fair, then if one approach fails you can try another. You can observe the effect that your words are having and adapt your style or approach accordingly. You can argue, cajole, pit your wits against those of your prospect. Naturally, you try to avoid the wrong initial approach. But because the prospect stares you (literally) in the face, you often have a second chance when the first proves unrewarding.

In that case, you sacrifice your own time in the hope of a direct sale. Unless the customer or the sale is important, the exercise is not worth your time. The beauty of a letter is that it can be prepared swiftly and cheaply. In return, you must watch your words with even greater care than if you were speaking. If your overture falls flat, you will get no encore.

Curiously, many top-selling organizations which work out a careful routine for their sales staff prepare little or none for their sales letters. Sales staff are taught what to say and how to say it, how to respond to each reaction of their customers, the precise approach to each stage of the selling process. They learn how to insert their feet in the doors of commerce and how to keep them there.

All this makes good sales sense. Why, then, do the same businesses become so sloppy when they take to the mails for sales? After all, it is much easier to provide drafts for letters than precedents for speeches. Reproduction on paper is far more certain than in either speech or procreation. If you are prepared to devote enough time and thought to your sales letters, you still will not be able to guarantee that they will 'click' every time, but they should give birth to far better results than you get at the moment.

What, then, should you include in your sales literature? Is yours a case for the soft sell or do you plunge right in and hit your customer hard? Do you make a special introductory offer or is yours a 'once only' effort? Do you lay emphasis on price or quality, on past achievements or future prospects. Should you adopt a style that is formal or colloquial?

Precisely because of the infinite variety of circumstances, products and services, of sellers and buyers, of needs and impulses, no one can answer these questions for you. You must do so for yourself.

So sales letters require thought and preparation. You should not 'bash out' a letter, 'tear off' a memorandum to a customer, 'dictate a quick "mailing shot" ' – and then have it completed and polished by some subordinate or maybe signed in your absence. These letters count. They must suit your purpose or they will not achieve it.

34

Applying for Posts – and Selling Yourself

As a preliminary to any legal arrangement, as an opener of the contractual door, as a means of getting a foot inside the boardroom, the office, the factory or any other place of work – the letter of application is crucial. Of all the business letters that you have to write, the job application is the hardest. You are selling yourself by direct mail, or at least using the mail to invite an offer for your services. So consider the best way to perform this immodest task.

What made you write? The answer provides a simple, brief, effective and invariable opening gambit:

I am replying to your advertisment in today's *gazette* ...

I understand from our mutual friend, James Brown, that you have a vacancy for the position of ...

I have been referred to you by ...

The chairman, managing director, company secretary, personnel director – the potential employers or their representative – will not at this stage toss your letter into the waste basket. The door is unlatched. Apply your shoulder:

I am most interested in the possibilities which your position offers.

I appreciate the responsibilities which the successful applicant would bear and I find these exciting.

The challenge offered by your post is one that I would welcome.

Members of Parliament, of local authorities and of the board of directors of companies all share a duty. They must declare any interest in matters under discussion. If, for instance, you have a financial interest in a contract which your board is considering, then you must say so. If you wish to win a place on that board and are applying from the outside, then the more interested you appear in the work that is offered, the more likely you are to get it. Employers seek enthusiasm.

So you have explained the origin of your application and your interest in the work. You have introduced the subject. Now introduce yourself:

> I am 35 years of age, and have been employed in responsible positions in the industry, ever since I completed my Doctorate in ... at ... University.

> I am present ... director of ... Ltd. You will appreciate, therefore, how vital it is that my application to you be treated in confidence, whatever its outcome.

> I have immense experience on every side of the trade. I worked my way up to my present position of ... from the very bottom.

> I am 29 years of age, happily married and have three children. My working experience has been varied. The last eight years have been spent as ....

If there are disadvantages in your background, then even these may be turned to account.

> Although I have no practical experience of the ... industry, the many years I have spent in ... and ... have provided me with a knowledge of potential markets which I believe you would find valuable.

> I started work immediately I left school. Happily, evening classes enabled me to acquire the necessary academic background. Essentially, though, my experience has been obtained in the practical field. It stretches over seventeen years and into every aspect of the business.

Note that the approach is positive. You do not start with an apology: 'I regret that I have no academic qualifications ... a minimum of practical experience ... no knowledge of your particular trade ...' This is fatal. There are rare products that are sold so softly that the 'spiel' begins in an apologetic tone. These do not include yourself. Show both honesty and an appreciation of your difficulties by including your demerits. Every really good job application combines the maximum of self-praise with the minimum of immodesty.

Avoid the following:

> If I am to be accused of immodesty, then so be it. I must tell you that I am

highly qualified for the job.

I do not wish to appear immodest but ....

Modesty forbids me to set out at length the full scope of my experience.

I do not wish to indulge in self-praise, but ...

False modesty is insincere. Apparent insincerity is death to the job hunter. If you cannot even put yourself across tactfully, how can you manage others, sell products or oraganize a business? So away with the pretences. Tell the truth about yourself, with confidence.

No one likes to buy rejects, unless, of course, they are very cheap. Everyone on the other hand, likes to think that a product is custom-made for them. Those who think they have beaten the queue – and the market – to their purchase are contented and satisfied buyers.

Selling your house or your business? Then obviously you would not wish it to appear to be a drag on the market. Lines which 'stick' are sold off cheaply in sales. Conversely, the best way to encourage a customer to buy is to indicate that the goods are in short supply. The retailer who puts a 'sold' sticker on an article is sure to get enquiries: 'Can you get one of these for me? Have you any more of these in stock?' One bright spark disposed of a line of really slow sellers by putting a large sign on the counter which read: 'Sorry – only one per customer'.

So your application must not appear shop-soiled. You must not be an apparent reject.

The higher the position you seek, the more important it is that you appear to be 'just the person we need'. While you are asking for the post, you must quietly indicate that the jobs crying out to be done by you. The salesman shouts: 'Last few only ... hurry and buy before stocks run out .... I can offer you a special, unrepeatable rate ...' The customer feels privileged, contented, eager to buy. That is the feeling that your letter must instil in your potential employer.

So include a *curriculum vitae* – separate from but attached to your letter. Make sure that key parts of it are in the letter itself (as in examples already given) and that you introduce it with care. Thus:

To avoid overloading this letter with details, I am enclosing an account of my background and experience.

I hope that the enclosed C.V. will be helpful.

I have prepared for you a brief account of my experience, background and personal details, which I enclose herewith.

Under no circumstances should the 'enclosed details prepared for you' appear to be duplicated. The extent of your lie becomes all too apparent. (Please do not laugh – I have seen this sort of error perpetrated dozens of times by job applicants who remain applicants always.) Personalize even the documents that are sent out to all and sundry. Re-angle them, re-type them, remodel the words, the introduction, the ending. Above all, be selective in the facts that you present.

Selectively is the key to successful self-marketing. Study your market. Read the advertisement. Find out what the company does. Put yourself in the place of the selectors. Ask yourself: 'If I were them, which details would I want? Which would I regard as unnecessary? Which facts would impress, which would depress? What should I include and what leave out?

You cannot always know the precise nature of the work you are applying for, or even of the business. Before you write, try to get some general idea.

I used to select staff for an organization which included in its name the words 'Bridge'. It had nothing whatever to do with card games, but every batch of applications contained at least one in which the writer praised his or her own skill as a card player. They brought a touch of hilarity to the selection board, but never an interview. Our advertisement was clearly worded, so the applicants' interpretation of it showed lack of either care or intelligence or both, and disqualified them for an executive position. If in doubt, they should have had the good sense to prevaricate or to check by telephoning before committing themselves to paper.

Now, there is a phrase which has become so commonly used that it has lost its true meaning. A pity, because it expresses it admirably. When you put your application onto paper, you commit yourself.

When you do come up for interview, you are almost certain to be asked why you want the job. Work out the answer before you apply for that interview or you may never get one. Ask what they want of you and see how you can best indicate that you are able to fulfil their needs. You are writing a sales letter, but you have special difficulty because your product is yourself.

How extraordinary it is that the same people who will spend many useful, thoughtful hours drafting letters for products or services will not spare a few minutes in order to do the same for their career prospects.

35

Interviews for Jobs

An interview is basically a one-sided negotiation which, both sides initially hope, may lead to a contract of employment. There are no laws which regulate the carrying out of that interview, but its outcome should always be confirmed by letter.

With luck, both sides will be satisfied. The prospective employer will offer a contract and the prospective employee will accept that offer. In any event, courtesy requires the employer to inform the interviewee of the decision taken. Interviewees who reject the job should write and say so.

If the employer has offered payment of expenses, then by coming to the interview the interviewee accepts that offer and those expenses must be paid. Otherwise, the law does not require prospective employers to pay for the interviewee's fares or meals.

Invitation to be interviewed

We shall be pleased to interview you for the post advertised. Would you please call at the company's above address and see our personnel manager, Mr Robert Jones, at 12.15 p.m. on Monday 18 July. If this time is impossible for you, please telephone Mr Jones and arrange another mutually convenient appointment.

I confirm that we shall be pleased to pay your fares and other reasonable expenses involved in attending the interview.

Application accepted

Thank you for attending the interview. Your application for the position of ... has been accepted. I shall write to you in detail within the next few days.

Application refused

I regret that it has not been possible to offer you the post for which you kindly applied. We were deluged by applicants, many of whom had more experience in the field than yourself. May we nevertheless thank you for your application and wish you every good fortune in the future.

Applicant rejects offer

Thank you very much for offering me the post of.... After anxious consideration, I have decided not to change positions at the moment.

Applicant rejects, again

My company has made me an offer which I find irresistible. In the circumstances, I have decided to stay on in my present post. Thank you for your kind offer and for the time which you gave me.

36

Retirement and thereafter

Retirement may mean exile to some seaside town or sheltered village. Too many professional and business people, though, are put out to grass when their appetite for work is undiminished and their desire for rest is as small as their need for money is great. They leave one position to hunt for another.

Many of the letters in Chapter 34 can do good service irrespective of the user's age. Here are some additional suggestions.

> I am retired, but not retiring. I have twenty years' experience of ... and I wish to continue to put it to good use.

> My company operates a compulsory early retirement scheme, so as to make way for the young. For this reason, and for this reason alone, I am now seeking alternative employment. My interest in my work and my ability to carry it out are equally undiminished.

> I am in far too good health to give up working, and I have several new schemes for improved production/data processing/personnel selection/ which I am looking forward to putting into effect.

> Since my compulsory retirement three months ago, I have had the opportunity to undertake refresher courses in computer programming, management methods and general business administration. These, combined with my forty years of active experience in the industry, make me anxious to begin my new career without delay. I would be happy to call on you.

> I am as physically fit as I am mentally restless, and I want to work in our industry.

> My younger colleagues and I worked in complete harmony. A rule which the company made inflexible in order to provide incentive and opportunities for them has resulted in my being forced into early retirement. Your company, I understand, is more concerned with mental agility,

physical energy and commercial experience than with age.

My years of experience being great, I trust that my years of age will not disqualify me from the post you offer. My expectation of active working life is at least another ten years. By then, I hope to have made a thoroughly firm and useful impact on your ... department/company.

It is true that I shall bring with me years of age but at the same time, I have an accumulation of knowledge and know-how, skills and experience which are probably unique in the industry. These have been acquired, as you know, in the service of ... Ltd. Owing to their compulsory retirement scheme, they have no further apparent use for my talents. I would greatly appreciate the opportunity of talking to you, and of indicating some of the respects in which I would hope to be of long-term service to your organization.

Please would you see me? I have some extremely interesting information which I would like to discuss with you. I am desperately upset at having been forced into early retirement, but the knowledge and know-how, skills and contacts acquired in the service of my former company will, I believe, be of great potential use to you.

Your letter must indicate active, youthful energy plus great experience. The very defects of age which have caused your dismissal may be your greatest assets. Avoid the miserable old phrases – 'I am a youthful 65', or 'I am an active, middle-aged person'. Be positive.

Are you applying for a position at a lower salary than you were previously enjoying? Then do not say: 'my needs are now much smaller. I am prepared to accept less than I previously got.' The former allegation is probably untrue and the latter is all too obvious.

Anyway, why should you not start climbing the ladder, once again? Many of the world's most successful people achieved their eminence long after companies retire their executives. De Gaulle, Churchill, Adenauer, Eisenhower, Reagan ...

37

To the press

Letters to the press are a democracy's safety valve. It may vent your frustration to write to the press, but it is also pleasant to see your views in print. Here's how:

1 Be concise. In spite of all the rubbish that gets published, the extraordinary fact is that nearly every paper (trade or commercial, local or national) is short of space. A rambling epistle gets spiked.

2 Avoid defamation (see Chapter 52). You may make 'fair comment on a matter of public interest'. You are entitled to express your opinion, but any facts upon which it is based must be substantially correct. The opinion need not be 'fair' in the sense that it is reasonable or sensible. The most outrageous views are entitled to (and often get) an airing on the letters page.

   Most editors are anxious to keep out of trouble with the laws of libel. One Sunday national rejected (and paid me for) a commissioned article on the ground that, although accurate, it might cause offence to people with whom they were anxious to keep on friendly terms. When I gently suggested that they were meant to be '*the* fearless paper', the then features editor replied, 'We must have a paper to be fearless in!'

3 The swifter your reaction to the news, the more topical your piece, the more cogent your reasoning, and, of course, the more highly respected and well-known your name or that of your organization, the better your chances of getting published. The letter itself makes news.

Another suggestion. It is often worth telephoning the editor or letters page editor of the paper and asking whether a letter on the subject you have in mind would have any reasonable chance of publication. There is rarely any guarantee that your letter will appear but if it has a blessing from the top the chances are good.

For the paper's opening and closing preferences ('Dear Sir' as opposed to 'Dear Editor', or perhaps, 'Dear John' – and 'Yours, etc.' as opposed to 'Yours sincerely', etc), see the column. If you want to sell (even for nothing), study your market. Fall in with the idiosyncrasies of the paper.

You are not of course expected to accept the views of the editor. Basically, there are two main sorts of letters arising out of editorial policy and a paper normally publishes examples of each. The first (well loved, naturally) is in sympathetic praise, and designed to encourage a continuation of the pressure and publicity already given. The other presents the other side of the coin.

> My company is deeply involved in the Smoke Town Development Scheme. It is vital for the future of this entire area. With it, adequate and varied employment is almost guaranteed. Without it, the stagnation from which this town has been suffering for a considerable time past will be exacerbated. Young people will continue to leave the area in search of better jobs. This in its turn will deepen the recession and depression which have in the past done much to keep new industry away.
>
> While appreciating the disadvantages which you so succinctly explained in your editorial, we are surprised that you do not appear to welcome the development as a whole. To find the local newspaper fighting local progress is sad indeed. We would at least like your readers to know that all criticisms of the development are most carefully considered; that we make every effort to produce schemes which will cause the least possible disturbance and the maximum advantages to the amenities of the neighbourhood; and that (commercial advantages apart) we believe that when this development is complete, the changes it will bring to the area will be welcome to all.
>
> Knowing the fair hearing which you give to those whose views differ from your own, I do hope that this letter will be published. We are anxious that your readers should understand that there is another side to the case.

Note:

1 Remember that the editor always gets the last word, so vituperation may not only keep your letter out of the column but also provoke a reply in kind, which may be more harmful to you than your aggressive approach was to the paper (or to the case which you were seeking to attack).

2 As in all aspects of life (commercial and private), aggression and hostility provoke like response. Attacks which are reasonably subtle, as well as civil and well reasoned, generally produce better results.

3 The letter on page 101 would be greatly strengthened if a paragraph could be added setting out (in brief, concise sentences), some of the facts on which the writer relies, to show that the development will help the area, and/or that care has been taken in its preparation.

In support of editorial policy

It was a pleasure to read the clear and concise explanation of the aims of the Smoke Town Development in your editorial. May we add one further word? We believe that, in the long run, the capital which will be attracted to this area will benefit not only the industries which will be represented on the new estate, but everyone in the county. A revived local economy combined with new and well-paid employment will bring money into the shops, work to those who provide services of all kinds and satisfaction to the local householders of every category. That, certainly, is our wish and that of all others concerned with this project.

Enclosing letter to editor – supporting paper's policy

We were delighted to read your editorial in your last month's issue and hope that you will find it possible to publish the enclosed letter in support. The development has so many detractors that were it not for your lively and helpful support, we would be very pessimistic about the future. Thank you, in any event, for your guidance and encouragement.

We would be very grateful if we could have 2,000 reprints of the editorial concerned. How much would they cost? If you could kindly get the appropriate person to telephone our Mr Jones this would be much appreciated by us all.

With renewed thanks and hoping to see you again soon, and with all best wishes.

Note:

1 A covering letter often helps. If you know the editor, so much the better. Even if the letter which you want to have published is an attack on editorial policy, a covering note can do no harm (see the example immediately following these notes).
2 Who should sign the letter? In general, the more weighty the writer's reputation, the more likely it is to be published. If the writer of the covering note is not the person who has signed the letter, explain why. (Again, see next example.)
3 Remember the reprints service that papers usually provide, willingly and at a low price. Reprints are often the most helpful, influential and cheapest form of public relations material.

Enclosing letter to editor– attacking paper's policy – from someone known to the editor

I am taking the liberty of sending you a letter from our Chairman, which we all very much hope that you will publish. We appreciate that it contains an attack on one aspect of your editorial policy, but we know that your shoulders are broad and that you are seldom unhappy when your editorials provoke a lively reaction! We would have preferred, of course, to have written in support of your policy, but know that you will not take it amiss if we hope that your views will not be immutable and that words of our Chairman may influence not only your readers, but (dare we hope) even yourself?

Anyway – and seriously – we would all feel much better if the other side of the case could be ventilated.

Meanwhile, my kindest regards and apologies for troubling you. With best wishes.

Note:

1 This letter is suitable for a public relations officer or less senior executive who is on friendly terms with the editor. The editor will, of course, realize that the letter signed by the big boss was probably drafted by the public relations officer or junior executive. No matter. This approach at two levels often achieves good results.
2 Do not forget to end with a friendly greeting.

Intelligent antagonists make a clear distinction between their regard for the editor and the paper and their poor view of the opinions they wish to attack.

Enclosing letter to editor – attacking paper's policy – from a stranger

I enclose a letter from our Chairman. I do hope that you will manage to publish it. There is extremely strong feeling here that it would be fair to give space to the other side of the picture.

I am asked to tell you, also, that if you or any of your staff would care to meet us, we would gladly make arrangements for a site visit. We feel sure that we could provide information and help which would assist you in what we appreciate is a difficult task.

Note:

1 Find out and use the editor's name. This distinguishes the covering note from the 'Dear Sir' letter for the column, and subtly flatters the recipient.
2 Editors are busy people, so the shorter and more pointed your remarks, the more likely they are to reach the boss's desk, rather than that of an assistant. Then, perhaps, your letter will reach the person in charge of the letters page with a recommendation from the top.

38

Congratulations and condolences

Sincerity is the keynote of the good personal letter. Slush is unpleasant for the feet in snowy times and revolting to the mind whatever the occasion. Here are some precedents of the few, appropriate, welcome words that a situation of joy or sorrow requires.

Congratulations

Well done! Myra and I were delighted at your good news. We wish you every good fortune.

Well done – but formal – on promotion

I have been asked by my Board to tell you how very delighted they were to read of your promotion. They wish you every success, and so do I.

On honour

Together with all your colleagues in the industry, we rejoice at your new distinction. We wish you many years of good health in which to enjoy it.

Recovery from illness

We were all delighted to hear that you are back in harness. Congratulations! We hope that you will now keep fit – and that you will resist the temptation to overwork.

Please join me for lunch, as soon as possible. Meanwhile, best wishes from us all.

Condolences

We were shocked to learn the tragic news. Your husband was a magnificent colleague and a man whose opinion, company and judgement we all valued. We shall miss him.

We all feel very helpless, but if there is anything that any of us can do to be of assistance, we would regard it as a favour if you would not hesitate to let us know. Meanwhile, my colleagues and I send our warmest regards and our most sincere sympathy. We share a deep feeling of loss, and trust that you will be spared any further sorrow for many years to come.

What can I say? We were all so very fond of Mary. I know that even though she had been suffering for so long – and to that extent, her passing must have been a merciful release for her – it must still have been agony for you to lose her. We would all like to be of help to you, if we can. Is there anything we can do? Please phone or write or call. We really would like to do something constructive, if possible.

It occurs to me that you might like some help with the legal miseries of winding up the estate or dealing with personal effects. If we can take any of these worries off your hands, please tell us and we will put the company solicitors at your service. Their probate department is very efficient.

Janet joins me in sending you our fond sympathy. We hope to see you soon.

The sad news of your husband's passing was received at Head Office today, and on behalf of the directors and the staff I send our sympathy to you and to your family in your loss, the sadness of which we share.

From the time your husband joined our company, he earned everyone's respect, and we have lost a valued colleague and friend.

As some measure of tangible help at this time, I must inform you that Mr Smith was a participant in our Staff Life Assurance Scheme. In due course, you will receive a cheque for £... from the Trustees of this fund.

Our insurance company will need a copy of the Death Certificate and probate of your husband's will. If Mr Smith left no will then Letters of Administration will be required. Your solicitors will advise you how to apply for these if that course is necessary, but if there is any help which I or my assistant, Mary Brown, can give you, please do let me know.

Note:

The formula for letters of condolence should be:

1 Sympathy.
2 Comfort – which includes words of praise for the deceased.
3 Offer of practical help – if possible, in concrete terms.

4 A touch of normality – including suggestions for future meetings, and even sometimes a small touch of humour.

5 Tact – which generally includes the avoidance of emotive words such as 'death'. 'Passing' is a fair substitute. Usually, you need not mention the circumstances giving rise to the letter. They will be only too painfully obvious. Do avoid pomposities like 'sad demise', 'tragic passing on' and 'the world to come'.

6 If you know that the survivor to whom you are writing holds strong religious beliefs, then write a letter such as that which follows. Otherwise, the words may be regarded as tactless (at worst) or cant (at best).

The comforts of religion

I know that Bob's life was given up to the service of other people – not least through our church. I am sure that the world in which his spirit now lives for ever will be one free of pain, where his good deeds, fine character and remarkable unselfishness will receive their reward.

Meanwhile, Jenny and I send you our most sincere sympathy. We would like to be of help in some way and as we are coming up to town next week, we will telephone to see if we can drop by for a chat. If we can be of assistance before then, we would be very pleased if you would contact us.

I need hardly say how shocked and upset we are at the news – but we are confident that, with God's help, you will find strength.

Our fondest greetings to you.

39
Thank you

Call it a 'bread and butter' letter, if you like, but there is none more important. People who consider that they are entitled to be thanked but who receive no words of gratitude may feel both angry and hurt, as may those who feel they have not been thanked adequately.

Thank you letters need not be long. They must be sincere and apt. They should preferably be handwritten (see Chapter 28) when they are personal – such as thanking the recipient for hospitality. But for business occasions they may be incorporated at the start, and probably repeated at the finish of an ordinary, routine letter.

Here are some thankful openings and closings:

My husband and I are very grateful to you for your hospitality, which we greatly enjoyed, and which we now look forward to returning.

We cannot thank you enough for the way in which you and your wife put yourselves out to make our visit to ... so happy and memorable.

We did enjoy the hospitality of your home, the company of your family and friends and the theatre evening which you arranged for us. We hope that it will not be long before you and your wife visit .... Our home will then be yours. We hope that you will feel as at home in it as you made us feel in yours.

It was a delightful lunch – which I enjoyed. It was a pleasure to break the business routine in your company and I am grateful to you for your time and hospitality.

Many thanks indeed for your courteous kindness to me when I visited your works.

My Chairman has asked me to say how greatly he appreciated the courtesy extended to him when he visited your factory. He will himself be writing to your Chairman, very shortly.

Your letter was immensely appreciated. Thank you so much.

It is no exaggeration to say that, thanks to you, yesterday was the most memorable day we have had for a long time.

I cannot resist the opportunity of expressing once again our appreciation for your courtesy and kindness.

We are very grateful to you for your help, which went far beyond the call of duty.

You have done us a very good turn – and we look forward to the chance of repaying our debt of gratitude.

We do appreciate your help and are grateful for it.

You are a good friend and your assistance was much appreciated.

It is really a delight to work with people who are not only colleagues, but also excellent friends. Thank you for ....

It is a pleasure to compete against you! Your courtesy and consideration last night were enormously appreciated.

Finally, we would like to express once again, our appreciation for ...

In conclusion, we send our renewed thanks for ....

With our renewed thanks and all best wishes.

Thank you once again for ....

Next, who better to thank than a grateful customer or client? Thus:

Your letter dated the ... has been received by the Managing Director, and she has asked me to write to you to say how grateful she and the other members of the Board are for your kind remarks.

We always do our best to ensure the satisfaction of our customers, but it gives us great pleasure when we receive letters of appreciation such as the one which you were kind enough to write.

My directors very much hope that our business relationship with you will continue for many years, to our mutual satisfaction. Your kind sentiments are being conveyed to .... and the staff at .... Thank you again for your trouble and thoughtfulness in writing.

So far, we have looked at letters of thanks for favours received. But offers may also be acknowledged with gratitude. Refusal may need to be both tactful and graceful. Here are some helpful fomulas:

It was extremely good of you to ask me to....I am very upset that I cannot accept.

I have tried hard to put off a previous engagement for exactly the same time as your..., but without avail. So I must refuse your invitation – but I do so with much regret and hope that you might ask me again another day.

My trouble is an overfull diary. I so wish that you had asked me just a few days ago. As it is, I have a prior appointment which I cannot possibly cancel.

How very good of you to invite us! And how very sorry we are to have to decline.

Once again, I fear, duty must come before pleasure. I cannot accept your invitation, because on that very day...

As our American friends put it, could I please take a raincheck on your invitation? I simply cannot get away from the office/works/factory/shop at the moment.

I do hope that you will not be offended at yet another refusal. Somehow, our meeting seems to be fated not to take place.

It is very kind of you to ask my wife and myself to visit you at home. But we both feel that this time the hospitality should be ours. As it happens, the date you mention is very difficult for us. May we instead suggest that we would welcome a visit from your wife and yourself to us on...

I am always happy to add profit to pleasure. Your suggestion of a business lunch next week is one that I would accept with alacrity, were it not that....As it is, please forgive me – perhaps our secretaries could fix another day, convenient to us both?

Then what of the guests who do you a favour by coming? The speakers or lecturers invited by you who give their time because they are fond of you, or need your goodwill? Or the colleague who works overtime to help you to replan your works? Or maybe your son or daughter, who deserves a pat on the back for some commercial kindness? All too often we forget that those closest to us are still entitled to our gratitude and that if they earn it, we are very lucky.

So here are some useful lines of appreciation:

You fill your time with service to others – and we are both proud and privileged that you spared your afternoon last week, to visit our...

We are extremely grateful to you for speaking to our staff/board/sales representatives/sales conference/management trainees. You will have noticed how attentive they were to your words. Perhaps the greatest tribute of all was the bombardment of questions, which you so skilfully answered and parried. It was with great regret that I had to conclude the meeting. We all hope that you will come again. Meanwhile, we do thank you.

No father is entitled to favours from his daughter/son – and that I get so many from mine really gives me enormous pleasure. Apart from being an honoured offspring, you are a good friend to your aged dad and I am grateful.

I do really appreciate, Father, the confidence you have placed in me. I am also grateful for the financial security which you have now given me. I shall do my utmost not to let you down.

I would like you to know how grateful I am to you for the help you have given to me in this very difficult period. We are now through the woods. I do not know how I would have survived if it were not for your support.

Finally, a word of thanks may serve as an important reminder. For instance:

Just a note to thank you very much for sparing me so much time during my recent interview. I greatly look forward to hearing from you.

It was very good of you to agree to.... We all look forward to your visit on.... I confirm the details, which are...

Thank you so much for saying that you would send me.... This will be immensely helpful.

It was very good of you to promise.... Your support/help/action will make all the difference.

40

Appeals

A successful appeal must have direct and personal relevance to the reader. The wealthier the recipients, and the greater their reputation for generosity, the greater the number of such letters they will receive. Benevolent millionaires have told me that they get hundreds of appeal letters every week. Naturally, most of the 'round robins' are consigned to the basket. Most replies must say 'No'. The appeals that produce results are usually personal, from people whom the donors do not wish to disappoint or whose requests they respect.

At best, the response results from true altruism. The cause is worthy and the giver is willing.

Often, however, self-interest plays its part. People like, for instance, to gain a touch of immortality for themselves or their families through the naming of a building or a bed, or an inscription in a book or on a roll of honour.

Then there is money. To earn you must spend. Those who send forth their bread upon the waters of charity may harvest some commercial gratitude. Call it sordid if you like, but when the chairman of your main customer company asks for a donation for his pet charity, can you refuse?

Anyway, you have your own pet project, haven't you? Doubtless the day will come when you will write to a friend or colleague who raided your pocket, saying, 'I am sorry to be a nuisance, but the cause is excellent'. They will sigh, reach for their pens and return the compliment. They are presidents or treasurers of their charities, you of yours. The cynic may have little use for either of you. But the organizers of the charity and (far more important) its beneficiaries, will bless you both.

We all want blessings and need them. Faith, hope and charity are the bastions of our world. The doing of good deeds and the giving of charity lie at the root of every religion, and even those who are irreligious may respond to non-secular appeals, just in case.

So successful appeal-makers have much in common with sales-people. They must study the market and frame and angle their letters accordingly. Each has his or her own methods. Study those of the successful and copy them. Before you criticise, consider the results.

A famous *schnorrer* – a Jewish beggar by a much kinder and more appreciative name – is said to have approached a leading Rothschild. 'Will you help me?', he asked.

'You know that I do my best not to refuse help,' replied the charitable magnate. 'But I really do feel that when you come to see me, you might at least wear clean and respectable clothing.'

The man looked down at his shabby garb and then up at his prospective benefactor. 'Mr Rothschild,' he said, gently. 'Do I presume to tell you how to run your bank? No. Then please do not tell me how to beg!'

So learn from others. Make a collection of the appeal letters, brochures and circulars that you receive. Ask yourself, 'Which ones strike home to me? Which have meaning and vitality? Which make me give?' When you know that, your research is becoming productive.

Usually, you will find that the letters which are really appealing combine sincerity, simplicity and personality. Their presentation is sufficiently unusual to remove them from the ruck. These will be enclosed with a personal note.

> As I expect you know, ever since we discovered that David had severe learning difficulties, Mary and I have thrown ourselves into the work of the Happiness Home. Unfortunately, the place is desperately under-staffed and cannot cope with half the children who need help. The greatest shortage is money. Please will you make a donation/join our organization/take an advertisement in our brochure/(or as the case may be)? Should you wish to contribute from a charitable source, the Registered Charity number is ...
>
> We do know the many calls that are made on your generosity, but this one is very close to us. Thank you so much.

Or:

> This is my year as chairman of the Trade Benevolent Fund. The need is enormous, as the enclosed pamphlet shows, and the fund does a vast amount of good. I hope that you and I will never need it, but many others do. I am enclosing a circular about ways in which you could help and I know that you won't let me down.

Or:

> We are desperately short of resources for our work. Please would you
> help? I look forward to hearing from you.

Or:

> Forgive this personal approach, but I do know the great interest you take
> in the Trade Benevolent Fund. If your company would help us this year,
> we would be immensely grateful. Your last year's contribution was
> £X,000. As we ran up a deficit of £Y,000 during the twelve months just
> ended, we are asking our contributors to be good enough to increase their
> donations. Would you please help in this way? The Fund really does do
> magnificent work – but it could not operate without the assistance of the
> leaders in the trade.
>   With all best wishes.
>   PS I have wrung the necks of my own Board, and I am happy to say that
> my organization will be doubling the contribution this year and donating
> £X,000, to set the ball rolling.

A few more rules, then:
1 The best fund-raisers are those who give – of themselves and of
  their money. They win by example.
2 Ask the recipients of your letter to write back to you personally –
  so that they do not think that they will get away with it by sending
  a miserable token to some anonymous appeals organizer.
3 Make things easy, if you like, by enclosing a reply-paid envelope.
  Never forget to send covenant forms, and/or to state the charity's
  registered number.

If ever you get stuck, find someone who is a successful fund-raiser,
ply him/or her with some judicious flattery – possibly washed down
with food and wine – and ask for help. Collecting money for charity
is a very big business: it is highly competitive and requires the best
organization. Nothing can beat a devoted angel at the helm.

Finally, a word from the head of a very generous charitable
foundation: 'When I receive beautiful brochures on splendid art
paper, I get cross and the charity generally gets nothing from me. If it
has that sort of money to throw away, then it cannot be as short of
funds as it says.'

The converse, from a rival philanthropist: 'You must spend money
to raise money. Unless you have a good-looking, well produced and
professional set of literature, I will not believe that you are a well and
professionally run charitable organization in which I should invest.'

There must be a happy medium somewhere.

41

Collecting for letterwriting

You may keep your own letters because you dream that one day they will be published. Dreams cost nothing, provided that they do not occupy too much space in your files or time in your day.

In general, though, it is a far more profitable occupation to collect the letters of others whose greatness is already known. Bearing in mind that the copyright in the collected correspondence of others rests with the writers (see Chapter 51), the words of the great have considerable value.

There are many dealers in manuscripts and autographs who make a good living by selling letters and autographs. You can collect the personal and public notes of kings, queens and princes. Some prime ministers' letters are surprisingly inexpensive; others are dear. The more famous the writer and the older and rarer the letter, the higher its likely cost.

Or specialize in literary letters. Many writers and poets of genius were also prolific and distinguished correspondents. There is nothing new about the letterwriter's art. In the days before telephone, telex or fax, the letter was the normal (and often the sole) means of long distance communication.

Remember, too, that letters were written long before the invention of postal services. Roland Hill invented the stamp but not the envelope. You may not be able to buy the original of the Epistle to the Corinthians, but you may discover a note from Napoleon. If the price is right, buy it. It should not only prove a splendid investment but will look good in a frame or album.

I know one couple whose lavatory walls are covered from floor to ceiling with the framed words of the great. Now, there's graffiti for you ... and what a marvellous way to ensure that both you and your guests may sit at leisure and contemplate your good taste.

It follows, naturally, that if you receive a letter from a famous personage you should keep it. If it comes to the company, you have no right to purloin it, but get permission from the top and this may be permitted. One reason why manuscripts are often marvellously underpriced is that their value is usually unrecognized – but now, at least, not by you.

Be careful before you throw out ancient letters from the loft. There, among the undiscovered Rembrandts, you may find some highly saleable scripts. Far more likely, there may be some ancient stamps on the envelopes. These may not prove as valuable as you had hoped. But if you keep the stamp on the cover and the cover on the letter, you may have a dusty goldmine on your hands. Anyway, a dream is still free and untaxable.

42

Occasions for letterwriting

It was an occasion of dread boredom. The dinner was bad, the company mediocre and the speeches dragged on towards midnight. Only one person at my table looked engrossed and happy. He was making notes of the speeches on the back of his menu card.

'Quotable material?', I asked him, when the evening eventually reached its morning end.

'That's what you were meant to think,' he said. 'Actually, my wife is abroad and I was writing her a letter!'

So I learned my lesson. When I am out speaking in public and someone scribbles at my side, I am not flattered. The diner or listener is probably writing a letter.

I have since taken a leaf out of that diner's menu card. Agendas and minutes, blank at the back, provide a monstrous temptation to scrawl a note of affection to far-off friends, or even a skeleton draft of a letter:

> I know that you will forgive the paper upon which this note is written, but at least it will indicate that I really am spending the time when you are away immersed in miserable business!
>
> You will see from the enclosed that where I am I wish I were not! Anyway, there is nothing like a touch of complete after-dinner boredom to provide the incentive for me to drop you a note, to thank you/to remind you/to commiserate ...

Of course, there are limits to the people who would regard this sort of note as a compliment. The same style and stationery that is ideal for close relations may destroy good relations with those who expect a more dignified approach.

So next time you are sitting on the platform listening to dull speeches or enduring wretched boredom at any sort of gathering, pick up your pen and the nearest available scrap of clear paper – and write.

'Someone has been messing with the duplicating machine again Miss Lindley?'

Part 5

SUPPLIES, SYSTEMS, STAFF –
AND MODERN TECHNIQUES

43

Stationery and supplies

Your letterheads, notepaper, compliments slips and other stationery are your literary shop window. If they are scruffy, inartistic or ugly, they will give a bad impression and harm you or your business. If they are neat, well laid out and handsome, your correspondence is far more likey to have its desired effect.

Why, then, do so many able people devote so little time and thought to their stationery? 'Oh, just order in some ordinary letterheads. Same as last year will do. Leave it up to the printers, they'll produce a design for us. Don't bother with proofs.' Fatal. If you want your letters to be telling, then they must be typed or written neatly and accurately on well designed and competently printed paper.

If you are in business, do you spend heavily on advertising agents, buying space in the media? Then why not spend a comparatively small amount on getting a professional designer to plan your stationery, or to redesign your logo? You would not begrudge the money if you were preparing a sales leaflet. So pay to sell yourself.

Cut the time spent by your staff and yourself on correspondence. The use of good precedents should help. Save through improving your word-processing and other systems of work or administration, but spend just that small amount more on the paper on which your letters are written. Even in the short run, the money should be well spent.

These suggestions apply, of course, to every sphere of both commercial and personal correspondence. They are especially relevant to letters concerned with the law. If you want credit to fend off legal proceedings brought by your debtors, then appear prosperous – which is impossible if you write on cheap paper. You wish to attract top management? Then give the impression that you operate a top outfit. Make sure that the design at the top of your paper will advertise your modern and business-like approach.

You would not allow your staff to look slovenly, when dealing with your clients or customers, would you? Then smarten up the stationery on which they present your written case.

44
The outside of the envelope

Appearances count and first appearances matter most. The scruffy, disreputable, uninteresting, poorly presented envelopes that first greet the recipients of too many letters do the writers no credit.

'I can't spend a fortune on envelopes of pristine white,' you say, trying to justify the miserable brown things in which you send out your mailshots. Nonsense. The top mail-order companies make sure that even if every letter is mailed by the thousand, each recipient feels that he or she is the one for whom it is intended (see Chapter 48 for more on direct mail sales).

Naturally there are limits to this doctrine. Nobody feels better about getting a bill just because it is in a splendid cover. Accounts should be sent out as cheaply and expeditiously as possible. But letters should be dealt with differently, even if they are requesting payment of accounts. They are part of the front of your business.

For mass mailings sticky labels can be useful. These computerized products of addressing machines should certainly be used for major list mailings, especially where the secretary or clerk will open the envelope and the recipient is unlikely to see it.

Where your letter is personal, have the envelope neatly typed. Note the form of title for the recipient (Chapter 8). Check that the name is properly spelt, and the address accurate.

If your letter is intended to be personal, mark the envelope accordingly. If you do not want the executive's secretary or the director's assistant to read the contents, mark the envelope 'Personal and confidential' or 'Strictly personal and private'. Underline it in red, if you wish. (For the legal implications of opening employees' mail, see Chapter 57).

If there is no indication that the contents are for the eyes of the named person only, you should not be surprised if anyone else in the business happens to open and read the letter. The great do not sort and sift their own mail. If your letter is intended for the personal attention of the addressee, then the envelope must say so. What is written on the envelope and the humble cover itself both matter far more than most letterwriters realize.

45
On files

There are several reasons for writing a skilful letter. First, you want it to have the appropriate effect on the recipient. That's the top copy. But the copy or carbon may be equally important. It will jog your memory about the contents, and it may be used in evidence, either at a hearing or in advance to show the strength of your case and so prevent a court action. Copies matter.

Of course, the finest, cleanest copy of the most brilliant of letters is useless if you cannot find it when required. So you need the most efficient filing system you can set up and operate.

Apart from the general rule that the simpler the system, the more effective it is likely to be, my advice is: devote time, thought and care to creating or adapting a system to suit your own needs. Commercial enterprises which depend so much on the accuracy of their records may spend millions on the development of their products but begrudge the few thousand pounds needed to establish a first class arrangement for their files. Of all business economies, this is the least intelligent, if only because a really good system will keep the filing itself to the minimum.

Simplicity, as always, is the key. At best, each letter will carry the reference number of the file and/or the reference of the matter in question (Chapter 5). If it carries neither, then the secretary or typist should be asked to put at the top right-hand corner of the copy some identifying number of reference which will make the finding of it child's play. If a bright youngster cannot operate your filing system, consider changing it.

46

Notes

Making and using brief notes can save the letterwriter a vast amount of time. If you write, type or word-process your correspondence, you can cast your eye back over the lines and amend, re-amend, excise or add as you see fit. When you are dictating onto a tape, it is aggravating to go back further than the last sentence or two. Notes are the answer.

The best system? Jot down at random ideas you wish to convey. Then put them into logical order. A one-word note should spark off a paragraph of dictation. The notes create the skeleton of the letter.

Notes should be concise. There may be some vital sentence that you need to work out in detail, but if there are many of these you would be better off dictating them (in logical order if you can) and then, if necessary, re-dictating from the first complete draft.

The first object of notes is to help you to structure a clear, concise and accurate letter incorporating the ideas that you want to convey. Their second purpose is to jog your memory. They need not be written at the same time as the letter. Carry a notebook or diary and practise jotting down ideas as they come to you – otherwise they will disappear, often never to return. These notes can be incorporated into those you make shortly before you write your letter.

In practice you will find the need for notes gradually lessens as your experience and skill increases. Once you are used to putting your notes into logical order and dictating them in letter form, you will find that you can sit back and put your thoughts into proper order without committing them to paper. The more flowing the letter, and the more polished your writing, the more likely it is that you will have mastered the art of using simple notes as indicators for complex thoughts.

Finally, you often need to make notes at meetings or even at meals to remind you of arrangements made with some other party.

Sometimes this can be left to an attendant secretary or scribe. Often you must do it for yourself, particularly if the meeting is private or informal. You must always make a note at the time: accuracy is important, and so is concentration.

How do you achieve precision in note-taking? Ideally, by using shorthand. The art of swift writing is too often regarded as the preserve of secretaries or professional shorthand writers. It is an enormous asset to anyone.

Even the simplest abbreviations help. Know the grammalogues – that is, tiny signs used for the most common words – and you can cut down your writing time by a quarter. Then leave out the vowels and another twenty-five per cent disappears. The words 'and', 'of', 'but', 'if', 'company' and the like, occupy an inordinate amount of space in ordinary script, so do 'public', 'private', 'board', 'director'...

A few hours spared to learn even the most basic shorthand can save hard and unnecessary labour, and add to the accuracy of your performance (see details and suggestions in the next chapter).

Learning to type or to word-process is more difficult and time-consuming. If you can handle a typewriter or word processor, you can bash out your own correspondence. Most executives used to leave this side of the business to the secretary or typist and many still do. But note-taking (preferably in shorthand) is a necessary chore for all. A good note has prevented many a bad letter.

These suggestions apply to every field of professional and commercial letterwriting. Barristers or solicitors who are able to take careful notes of a judgment, in shorthand which they can read and transcribe, are blessed. Architects or surveyors who are able to jot down the requirements of their clients swiftly and accurately will not only save time, but will also please their clients, whose precious moments are also spared. Doctors use their own form of shorthand for most of their reports. So should you.

47

Abbreviations, shorthand and letters to yourself

You can teach yourself all the shorthand you need in odd moments. My unpatented quick shorthand method requires no teaching whatsoever.

First, omit every vowel. Not for nothing did the Hebrews invent a system of writing where the vowels were inserted above and below the letters only in case of doubt. In most instances vowels are completely unnecessary to understanding.

Next, evolve your own system of abbreviations. Words most commonly used can be replaced by letters or signs. Ten minutes' thought can produce your own list, for instance:

'C' = the company; 'P' = product; 'Pt' = profit; 'L' = London; 'Bd' = board; 'F' = factory; 'S' = shop; 'O' = order.

Take any of your files and work out the words which appear most often. Consider the items which you write out in full which could be abbreviated without difficulty. Create your own shorthand.

Then buy a book on teaching yourself shorthand. Ignore the lines and twists, the signs and circles which can help you to build up whole words – you will have retired from the unequal battle long before you have perfected this system. Instead, just learn the few quick symbols for the most common words in the language. Pitman's method, for instance, uses grammalogues thus: a full stop for 'the' where not attached to another word; a tiny circle on the line for 'is'; a short, diagonal line for 'of'; and so on. The reduction in writing time achieved by using these few signs is great, the time required to learn them small.

Finally, abbreviate some prefixes and suffixes: '-ion' becomes 'n'; 'super-' becomes 'sr'; and so on.

And that is all. You now have a system of shorthand that is adequate for most purposes. You have worked it out in a couple of hours and perfected it in a week. You have saved yourself countless hours of unprofitable effort.

Naturally, you can afterwards dictate from your notes. You may even be able to train your secretary to read your shorthand. Why not? Plenty of secretaries read back each others' notes. Teach your shorthand to your children at college, and instead of writing to you once a month, they will be able to write once a week with precisely the same enthusiasm (or lack of it). They will also be able to make notes in classes and lectures with maximum speed. For this they will bless you – and blessings from our children are not lightly to be turned aside.

What, then, of the ordinary, humble abbreviation commonly used in commercial correspondence? There is a list of them in Appendix 2. Do not despise them. Abbreviations are a form of shorthand, accepted in the business world. They save time, effort and paper – provided that they are used accurately and sensibly.

48

Selling by mail

'Direct mail' means selling through the post. The cost is high: printing, postage, stationery, addressing and 'stuffing' envelopes, and building up, buying or renting lists of customers or clients. So the letter itself must strike with swift and unerring aim or the excercise will prove a costly failure.

Place yourself in the role of recipient. When you receive a mailing shot, why and when do you read it – and what makes you buy?

As with all letterwriting, the look of the envelope must be right. You must consider its colour and quality, the style of address, and whether a computerized label will suffice.

If you are writing to a company, then whom should you try to reach? The managing director, company secretary or buyer, the works, personnel or shop manager – or who else? As with all selling, you must identify your market and zoom in on the individual who has the authority to place the order. If you can target the person by name then do so, but make sure that you get the name absolutely correct. Otherwise, stick to the title:

'Dear Colleague/Delegate/Buyer/Executive/Fellow Manager...'

You may be lucky and have your own list of potential buyers. Perhaps you have built it up from previous business. Remember, though: people change jobs within organizations and move to other companies. Your own lists need frequent updating.

The next problem is how to start your letter. If you are using a word processor (see Part 6) you may start 'Dear Mr Brown' and then the machine can do the work for you. Otherwise you may address the shot to the managing director and start your letter 'Dear Sir or Madam'.

What should you put into the letter and what is better in an enclosure? Basically the letter should be brief and the accompanying literature should contain the detail. The letter must draw the customer's attention to the enclosure – and, with luck, to the order form.

The letter itself should be brisk. As always, the first sentence is crucial. Get that wrong and you pronounce the final sentence on the letter. Conversely, if you get the initial impact right you will arouse the interest of your reader and perhaps be on the way to a sale.

The first sentence should encapsulate the purpose of the letter. Tell the reader what you are offering and why it is unique.

You could pay professional copywriters to prepare your letter, but there are few who do the job really well. Even if they are craftsmen with words, they will know neither the product nor the market as you do. The best way is to do the job yourself and save the cost of the experts. If you have to use them, at least prepare drafts, review their rewrites and always insist on seeing the final draft and, if it is to be printed, a proof.

End on a climax, round off with your sales pitch. Sign. Then add a P.S. This has the next best impact to the first sentence.

Make sure that your reply card or order form is detachable; that any offer you make is easy to accept; that any reply is kept simple; and that the letter is accurate, well presented and professional. The sales letter must refer to the enclosures. The higher the aim the more dignified and prestigious the stationery and the wording should be.

Will the letter work? Try a test mailing and find out.

Which lists best suit your purpose? Probably those which you have yourself built up of old and satisfied customers and friends. Otherwise try local sources: the telephone directory; classified sections; trade directories; town guides; lists which chambers of commerce may provide, free or for a fee.

On the national level, use telephone and trade directories: *Kelly's 1,000* provides details of leading business enterprises, and the *Guide to Key British Enterprises* selects some 10,000 of the same. The *British Middle Market Directory* lists some 13,000 names.

If you are aiming at a specialist market you will find that most have at least one specialist directory. Professional, learned and other bodies, institutes and societies produce their own registers.

Other markets require other methods, for instance spotting from the electoral register young people who will be 18 that year, or checking engagements and marriages in the columns of the local paper.

You may also buy or rent lists from direct mail houses or other specialized organizations. Others will sell you their lists at a fee or even swop their list for yours. At the end of this chapter is a list of some of the organizations which may provide you with the help you need, from whom you may buy directories or lists, or from whom you can at least obtain guidance or quotes.

Remember, direct-mail selling is a highly skilled and competitive affair. Before you launch into it, work out the costings. How much will you have to spend and what return will make the outlay worthwhile? What are the current postal rates, how are they likely to change, and what are the maximum sizes and weights of mailing shots?

Would it be worth your while to arrange for sampling, testing or market research to be carried out before you make your investment? Letterwriting on a major scale involves massive potential expense and risk.

The same rules that apply to direct mail in the UK apply with even more force to direct mail overseas. The costs are higher.

At home or abroad, then, direct-mail selling is a professional business. If you are an amateur, take heed and advice before you plunge yourself and your fortune into this useful and growing but potentially perilous area of the letterwriter's art.

Useful publications

Sell's Directory of Products and Services
Sell's Publications Ltd, 55 High Street, Epsom, Surrey KT19 8DW
(Tel: Epsom 26376)

Kelly's Manufacturers' and Merchants' Directory,
Kelly's Directories
Windsor Court, East Grinstead House, East Grinstead
West Sussex, RH19 1XA
(Tel: East Grinstead 326972)

Guide to Key British Industries
Dun & Bradstreet Ltd,
26-32 Clifton Street, London, EC2P 2LY
(Tel: 01-377 4377)

Kompass Register of British Industry and Commerce
Kompass Publishers Ltd,
Windsor Court, East Grinstead House, East Grinstead,
West Sussex RH19 1XA
(Tel: East Grinstead 326972)

List of Commercial Directories
List of Surveys Ltd,
Bridge House, Station Approach, Great Missenden,
Bucks HP16 9A7
(Tel: Great Missenden 064271)

The Standard Industrial Classification
Her Majesty's Stationery Office (HMSO)
PO Box 276, London, SW8 5DT
(Tel: 01-873 9090)

The Direct Mail Databook
Gower Publishing Co. Ltd,
Gower House, Croft Road, Aldershot, Hants GU11 3HR
(Tel: Aldershot 331551)

The Postcode Address File
Postal Marketing Department (PMk 2.3)
Postal Headquarters, 33 Grosvenor Place, London SW1X 1PX
(Tel: 01-235 8000)
(Or contact the Postal Sales Representative at your local head PO.)

Useful addresses

The Direct Mail Sales Bureau plc
14 Floral Street, London WC2E 9RR
(Tel: 01-379 7531)

The British List Brokers Association
Springfield House, Princess Street, Bedminster, Bristol, BS3 4EF
(Tel: Bristol 666900)

The Direct Mail Producers Association
34 Grand Avenue, London N10 3BP
(Tel: 01-883 9854)

International lists of companies (ranked by size)

The Fortune World Business Directory. This lists the largest 500
industrial companies outside the USA plus 50 of the world's largest

banks ranked in order of turnover in dollars.

The *Double 500*. Published in two parts in May and June each year, showing the first 500 and the second 500 of the USA's largest companies.

The *Times 1000*. Includes a list of 500 leading European companies. Available from Times Newpapers Ltd, 16 Golden Square, London W1R 5BN. (Tel: 01-434 3767).

Both the above are available from *Fortune Magazine*, Time-Life Building, New Bond Street, London W1Y 0AA. (Tel: 01-499 4080)

International directories

Kompass, a comprehensive directory of industry, trade and services elaborately cross-referenced. Company information includes capital, number employed, names of one or more directors, list of activities.

Directories exist for Australia, Belgium, Denmark, Germany, Austria, Finland, France, Holland, Hong Kong, Indonesia, Italy, Japan, Morocco, Norway, Singapore, Spain, Sweden, Switzerland, Taiwan, Thailand.

Available from: Kompass Publishers Ltd, Windsor Court, East Grinstead House, East Grinstead, West Sussex RH1 1XD.

Dun & Bradstreet European Market Guide contains details of line of business and credit appraisal of 300,000 concerns in 19 European countries. Published in three volumes. Also, *Latin American Guide, South African Market Guide*. Available from Dun & Bradstreet Ltd, 27 Paul Street, London EC2A 4JU.

Other useful addresses:

The European Direct Marketing Association (EDMA), The Secretary, HR Waldmeier, Fuchsenbergstrasse 15, CH-8645 JONA, SG, Switzerland.

Direct Mail Marketing Association Inc., 6 East 43rd Street, New York, NY 10017, USA.

49

Secretaries, dictating machines and other aids

When the typewriter and shorthand came in, the art of calligraphy went out. As executives' responsibilities increased, so the labour of committing words to paper was passed on to secretaries and shorthand typists.

Then along came the dictating machine and the word processor, and audio typists took over a major part of secretaries' work, while shorthand typists disappeared. So consider how to make the best use of all these aids to letterwriting.

Naturally, you need spares for your equipment. Strangely, the same business people who ensure as a matter of course that spare parts are available for their works machinery are often incredibly mean when it comes to their own office equipment. Most systems are well engineered and reliable, but from time to time they collapse. To operate a successful word processor or dictating machine system, you must have 'swops' to hand. And of course you need swift and reliable service engineers.

Shop around very carefully before you plump for any particular make. Once you have chosen, you are probably landed with it forever. Nothing is more aggravating than to have different machines in the same office or group of offices. Secretaries or copy typists fall ill. Then tapes may have to be sent to others for transcription. Machines break down. Then you will want only one set of spares.

Which equipment should you choose? All depends upon your needs, your pocket and your preference. Recommendation is important. Experience should be a good guide. For ideas, try purchasing the various office equipment journals, sent in most cases at no extra cost.

So much for the basic equipment of the letterwriter. Now for some hints on its use.

There is only one way to make a dictating machine your ally and that is to use it. At first, talking into a microphone and flicking a switch for a replay seems strange, but it is well worth the effort.

It is essential, of course, to have the right equipment, in decent working order and adequately supplied with spares.

Whatever machine you use, you will soon acquire your own technique. Writing a letter by machine takes practice. You will find that your ideas gradually fall into proper shape as you go along.

If the letter is complicated you should certainly jot down notes (see Chapter 46). If you are blessed with shorthand you may want to rough out the letter fairly fully and then dictate it. In many cases a precedent book may help your dictation to be smooth and unworried. At worst, remember that it is far better to dictate a draft and hack it about after typing and redictate, than to use longhand. Apart from the reduced physical effort involved, the result is generally more satisfactory and almost invariably less time-consuming. And what have you to offer that is more valuable than your time?

Techniques of dictation vary. Some people dictate even the punctuation. Others leave it to the transcribers. Some dictate slowly, others at great speed. Some are blessed with transcribers who can type swiftly and consistently from tape. Other typists are slower.

You should speak clearly, and give precise instructions. The nature and extent of these will depend on the skill and experience of the person who listens to your words. For instance, you should be able to say simply: 'Please see the precedent at page ... of the precedents book and adapt it to be sent to Messrs Smith & Co ...The amount involved is £300 ...Omit paragraph four ...Sign off with a paragraph inviting him to lunch ... and send my greetings to his wife ...' Or: 'Please use precedent No. 85 in the Letter Book – but you sign it on my behalf ...'

In some cases you will have to spell out words. 'I spell: Rumpleforth ... R-U-M (as in mother) -P (as in Peter) -L-E-F-O-R-T-H.'

To be sure that you have clearly expressed your meaning, say, 'I repeat ...', and then respell. If you do not include the words 'I repeat', you cannot blame the transcriber if the same words are typed twice.

One of the greatest risks in using a tape is that the contents are so easily erased. It is aggravating to have to redo correspondence because, having forgotten to remove the tape from the machine, you have rewound and then redictated over it. It is even worse if the tape goes astray and never gets typed. The entire office frantically plays back every reel or cassette they can lay their hands on in a desperate (and probably vain) attempt to trace the missing one.

So if you operate dictating machines, you must find some system to indicate when a tape has been used, and put it into its box with a slip or sticker indicating the contents, and perhaps the date.

Part 6

WORD PROCESSING

50

Word Processing and modern technology (by David Roth)

Do I need a word processor?

It has become almost impossible to pick up a newspaper or trade magazine without being bombarded by companies informing you that your letterwriting would be far more efficient if you had a word processor – or, a better one than you are using. Will the word processor you choose for your business live up to the advertiser's claims?

A word processor will help speed up day-to-day correspondence in numerous ways. It will make corrections easier, although these can be done relatively easily with a self-correcting electronic typewriter. On the whole, the most effective use of a word-processing system is for repetitive work, where sections of the text are used in several different documents. These can be installed in the memory and subsequently slotted into the appropriate sections of a particular document, which avoids the constant retyping of practically identical copy.

The word processor has the added bonus of allowing the printing of many perfect copies with minor changes (for example, a different address, name, final sentence, etc.) in a fraction of the time it would take using a normal typewriter. The most common uses for a word processor are standard letters, reports, legal documents, records, proposals, and mailing lists.

Standard letters

Standard letters are used for everything from reminder letters to overdue accounts to personalized mailing shots, or for most types of letters for advertising or marketing. The standard part of the text is printed out and the system automatically merges the names and addresses, which are stored in the machine, inserting them at the appropriate points in the text.

Reports and legal documents

If you produce long reports which then go through a number of draft stages, a word processor will save you and your secretary much proof-reading and retyping time. The first draft is typed into the word processor, a copy printed out and a record of the report stored in the computer's memory. The author then corrects, edits and adds to the draft, then returns it to the secretary who recalls the draft onto the computer screen and keys in the corrections as required. The printer then produces either another draft (some systems print a symbol indicating the alterations in the margin or mark the text in some way, to speed up the final checking), or a final report with any changes in the typestyle, spacing and layout. This has advantages both to the typist and to the author. The main ones are:

1 Only the corrections need to be typed in. The remaining text is untouched, and so does not have to be retyped and rechecked.

2 The author can make changes which previously would have caused a retype, and still get the work returned quickly. For example, the writer can insert new sections or paragraphs or delete unwanted ones or refine existing text. The secretary types new words into the machine rather than retyping old ones. The author can obtain a high-quality result remarkably quickly.

Updating

Word processors are invaluable for any text that requires frequent updating, for example sales manuals, price lists, brochures or mailing lists. Only the changes need to be retyped.

When is a word processor not a word processor?

If you are not already confused by the time you have made a few preliminary enquiries, you will certainly end up thoroughly perplexed by the many different word processing facilities and machines available. So here is a brief introduction to what a word processor is and the different forms it takes.

All word processors include the same basic components: a keyboard similar to a normal typing keyboard for inputting information; a printer for printing out the final result; an internal memory for storing text on some form of magnetic storage, either tapes or disks; and a working memory.

All models have visual display units (VDUs) like a normal TV screen. These vary in size, but generally display 20-25 lines of text.

This enables text to be seen as it is being typed in, or as it is recalled from the memory to be corrected and edited before printing. The computer world has yet to standardize its terminology for the various types of word processor, but here are some of the terms used:

The dedicated word processor

This is an integrated system used exclusively for word processing.

Word processing on computers

There is a vast number of word processing packages available for micro- and minicomputers. This could well be a solution if you do not have enough suitable work to occupy a word processor full time, as you would be able to combine other facilities with it, such as accounts, invoicing and stock control.

A Networked Computer System

This has a central storage area and can allow the sharing of printers. It has the advantage of having intelligent terminals, which can be individual micro computers, each with at least a working memory of its own, and sometimes external storage, so that work can continue for some time if the central storage device fails to function.

Storage

How much a word processor can store and the extent of its facilities are of great importance. Some machines are not easy to expand should you underestimate the storage size you require. In some cases you have to buy extended memory capacity to fulfil this requirement. A correct choice at the outset can save you much money. Word processor storage facilities basically fall into four categories.

1 The 3½" micro floppy disk
2 The 5¼" mini floppy disk
3 The 8" standard disk
4 The (Winchester) hard disk

In principle, the larger the disk the greater the capacity for storage. A single-density mini floppy disk stores about 30-35 pages of A4 text; a double-density mini floppy disk about 63-67 A4 pages; a single-density 8-inch disk about 100 A4 pages; a double-density 8-inch disk double that; whilst a hard disk stores about 3,500 A4 pages.

The hard disk, as well as having a higher storage capacity, is about ten times as fast in accessing information as any of the other systems, and has proved to be on the whole more reliable. Naturally, it is not cheap. If your budget is limited, your choice lies between 8-inch and 5¹/₄-inch disks. Some elementary calculations on your own workload will show whether 5¹/₄-inch disks are too small for your requirements. If you have reports to be typed which are longer than 60 pages, then the 5¹/₄-inch disk will have its disadvantages. This is a question of economics, but you would be well advised to take a long-term view of your typing requirements.

The Printer

There is no point in saving text and editing it only to view it on your screen. So a printing device is essential. The type of printer you choose will again depend largely on the application you have for it. There are four types of printer available:
1 The dot matrix printer
2 The character (daisy wheel) printer
3 The ink-jet system
4 Page printers

Dot matrix printers

The dot matrix printer works by a series of small pins (from 9 – 24 pins) hitting the paper to form characters. At the lower end of the scale they are reasonably fast and cheap, but do give a rather 'dotty' appearance and are noisy. Whilst this is adequate for internal use, it is less sharp and clear than the type from a normal typewriter with a carbon ribbon. However, 24-pin printers, which are more expensive, will produce far better results.

Daisy wheel printers

These will produce results comparable to that of a typewriter and work on the same principle, i.e. characters coming into contact with a carbon ribbon which in turn makes an impression on the paper. They are considerably slower than dot matrix printers and are noisy, but an acoustic hood can be purchased which will cut out a lot of the noise.

Ink-jet systems

The ink-jet printer works by spraying ink onto paper to form characters. It has the capability of printing in different type faces, as well as doing complicated graphics and is much quieter than a dot matrix or character printer. Some early models required 'special' paper.

Page printers

These are based on a similar technology to photocopiers and utilize either laser or liquid crystal arrays. The results achieved are excellent and they are very quiet. Currently, they are expensive and most are only able to print on A4 paper.

Whichever printer you choose speed is a most important consideration. In computer terminology this is measured in the characters per second (cps) or in pages per minute in the case of laser printers, it is able to print. The speeds available are between 20 and 450 cps. Generally, the more cps, the more expensive the printer. However, a speed of less than 50 cps would be unacceptably slow.

If you intend to print many standard letters or long reports, you will probably require an automatic sheet feeder to be attached to your printer. This is a device which clips on to the printer to enable it to take about 200 sheets of paper, feeding them into the printing carriage one at a time without any manual assistance. These are available as single or twin bin, twin bin being able to hold two different types i.e. letterheads and plain A4. If you do need this facility, be sure that the printer in which you are interested is able to take one, as not every printer can.

When buying a printer you must remember that it is the speed at which it prints a page that has the greatest effect on the amount of work that your word processor can handle in a day. For example, a 55 cps printer will take 2 hours less on a day's work than one running at 35 cps. A speed of less than 44 cps should only be considered if the workload for the word processor will never exceed half a working day.

So choose your printer with the utmost care. A wrong choice could lead to a frustratingly slow volume of work output and cause you and your organization tremendous difficulties.

Maintenance and after sales

Once you have bought your computer, you should receive the same attention from the seller's representative (often referred to as a 'dealer') as you did before the purchase was made. The dealer may provide a degree of free training to you as the user, though this varies considerably from dealer to dealer. If training is not included in the purchase price it is imperative that this is arranged separately in order to get the most out of your investment. Your word processor should also include a well documented manual explaining the entire system and all its commands, together with examples.

When your word processor is installed and in full operation, any breakdown is likely to cause severe disruption to your workflow. If the machine is new, you may have two remedies:

1 The agreement with the seller may give you express rights – either against the seller or under a 'guarantee' or 'warranty' against the manufacturer.
2 In any event, the Sale of Goods Act gives you the right to a word processor which is 'of merchantable quality' – that is, not defective – and 'reasonably suitable for the purpose supplied'. It is most unlikely that any clause excluding those rights would be upheld. If you are a private buyer, then any such clause would be void; and even in a business contract a court may hold such a clause to be 'unfair' or 'unreasonable' and hence unenforceable.

So if your machine breaks down you should be entitled to require the seller to put it right. In theory, at least initially, you should not need a maintenance contract at an additional charge. You may well be asked to pay between 10 and 15 per cent of the purchase price for a year's maintenance. But why should you pay this in order to remedy defects which should not have been there in the first place?

However, some people do take out a contract to avoid potential legal hassle. If you do want a service agreement, either from the beginning or for when the machine needs maintenance or repair as a result of 'fair wear and tear', shop around for the best deal.

Some suppliers offer a replacement machine; others do not. You should expect a normal response time to breakdowns to be under 24 hours.

Be careful that the maintenance contract does not commit you to obtaining consumer durables such as ribbons, disks and replacement print heads. There are now many alternative sources of supplies and you do not want to be tied down to any one supplier. Specialist consumables suppliers may charge as little as half as much as equipment suppliers.

Like any good insurance policy, your annual maintenance contract charge may be high, but the risks involved in not having one are usually greater. Many engineering companies will charge a high fee to service a machine not covered by a maintenance contract.

Remember that if the machine on which you rely breaks down, especially in a busy period, the result could be disastrous, so you will need not only facilities for prompt maintenance, but also possibly a back-up machine during the repair period.

Do word processors need a special environment?

Long gone are the days when computers required a room to themselves, special lighting, highly sophisticated air conditioning, and the like. Still, some environmental aids will help in the smooth running of your word processor.

Lighting

To get the best definition from the screen, lighting should be less bright than normal and should not shine directly onto the screen. Place the work station so as to avoid any reflections from nearby windows or from direct overhead lighting. Each desk should have its own lighting which can be adjusted by the operator to best advantage. Should glare be unavoidable, you can buy a variety of anti-glare filters and screens.

Electronic mail and facsimile

Word processing initiated the entry of computers into letterwriting. The technological revolution continues. Computers have now converged with telecommunications, enabling letterwriters not only to process their correspondence on screen, but to send it more efficiently as well.

Your correspondence may be word processed, and your organisation's records stored on disk. But is your computer linked to a telephone?

You can, with the help of a "modem", send your correspondence by phone, providing that the recipient has compatible machinery. You need not necessarily print your letter on paper, nor do you have to send it by post. You – or your secretary – simply presses a button, and your message is instantaneously transmitted.

Alternatively, you can subscribe to Telecom Gold or other international telecommunications networks, all of which provide a variety of "Electronic Mail" services.

While "on screen" correspondence is a popular form of in-house communication, most organisations use "fax" machines to correspond externally. You no longer need to wait anxiously for documents to arrive – your facsimile will transmit your letter immediately and accurately. Take care though to ensure that the recipients confirm that they have received your letter. It is as easy to say "I never received your fax" as it is to say "the letter is in the post".

Part 7

THE LAW ON LETTERS

Introduction

If you write letters, especially in business, you cannot avoid potential or actual contact with the law. The following chapters set out the laws that you are most likely to encounter, and explain how best to keep those brushes to the minimum.

First come those laws which apply specifically to letters: the legal implications of signing a document; the possible effects of carelessness in what you write; copyright; defamation; and other legal traps. Next, are the branches of the law which the letterwriter most commonly requires, for instance contracts in general and contracts of employment in particular. Finally, there are the vexed questions of suing for money you are owed; problems in court; and letters in dispute.

If you follow the legal rules set out in these pages, they should help you to keep as far away as possible from courts and tribunals.

'I take it you are familiar with the termination clause in your contract of
employment, Hopgood?'

51

Copyright

The ownership of a letter passes from the writer to the recipient. The letter you receive becomes your property. You may file it or tear it up, treasure it or give it away, but you are not entitled to copy it. Copyright remains with the writer. You cannot include the letter in your memoirs without the writer's permission. The laws of copyright are complex. Here is a summary.

Copy one person's work, goes the old saying, and that's cheating. Copy more than one person's efforts, and that's research! As far as the law is concerned, however, if you copy something in which copyright subsists, you are liable to be sued for infringement of copyright – and the more people's work you copy, the more potential plaintiffs you are creating. In daily office practice, however, we all work from precedents. Indeed, with modern, sophisticated equipment, copying becomes daily an easier task. But it has its perils. So consider for a moment the Copyright Designs and Patents Act 1988.

Where copyright subsists in any work, you are in general only entitled to copy that work with the licence of the owner. If you invent your own precedents, write your own advertising material, draw your own plans, diagrams and maps, or create your own instructions to your staff, you have the right to prevent them from being copied by others without your consent. Conversely you are only entitled to reproduce the original brain-children of others with their consent.

Copyright subsists in 'literary, dramatic, musical' and 'artistic and graphic works'. These terms cover just about everything, from railway timetables through drawings, maps, charts and plans to poetry and literature of the highest order. During the author's lifetime and for fifty years from the end of the calendar year in which the author dies, reproduction is usually only allowed with the author's consent. Nor need the reproduction be exact in order to amount to a 'copy' – a 'copy' is that which comes so near to the original as to give to every person seeing it the idea created by the original. So not only are exact reproductions covered but so are 'colourable imitations'.

Now, 'copyright' means the exclusive right to copy the work, to issue copies to the public, to perform or show (in the case of music, plays and films) the work, to adapt it, or to license or authorise anybody else to do any of these acts – usually in the United Kingdom or countries with reciprocal rights. But who is 'the owner'?

In general, 'the author of a work is entitled to any copyright subsisting in that work'. But there are exceptions – notably under Section 11 of the Act: 'Where a literary, dramatic, musical or artistic work is made by an employee in the course of his employment, his employer is the first owner of any copyright in the work subject to any agreement to the contrary.'

Before the 1988 Act, there was another important exception – where a photograph, portrait or the like was commissioned for payment, the person who commissioned it became the copyright owner. Now the new law gives copyright to the photographer or artist (unless agreed to the contrary). But the subject of the photograph or portrait has an important protection: where the work was undertaken for private and domestic purposes (like wedding photographs), the person commissioning the work has a right to prohibit publication.

All this is subject to agreement to the contrary. If you decide to have your office rebuilt or redesigned and you commission architects to draw up the plans, they normally retain the copyright. The fact that you commissioned and pay for the work is irrelevant. You are not entitled to take their designs, reproduce them and sell them – or even to reproduce and keep them. They have the right to decide who may and who may not copy the work.

There is nothing to prevent you from employing architects on the basis that you will acquire the copyright in their drawings – nothing, that is, except possibly their reluctance to agree to this.

Equally, if you employ talented people in your office on the basis that they will have copyright in any original works they produce in the course of their employment, the Act does not remove that right. Like so many pieces of legislation, it only applies in the absence of some agreement to the contrary.

What of employees whose literary creation belongs to their employers? Authors now have a new and significant right – a 'moral right' as it is described by the Act – to be identified as author whenever the work is published commercially, and the same is true of musical compositions broadcast in public. But this important right does not apply to one category of authors or composers: those whose works are owned by their employers because of their contracts. So employees are no more protected than before.

Chapter II of the Act lays down how copyright is infringed: if, without the licence or authority of the copyright holder, you copy the work (with limited exceptions for private research), or issue copies to the public, or perform, broadcast or adapt it.

There are exceptions. Libraries have special privileges. So do those who use extracts from works for the purpose of reviews or criticism or for the setting (and answering) of examination questions. In general, though, the rule is simple – literary, musical, artistic and architectural piracy are not permitted.

52

Defamation – the laws of libel and slander

It is defamatory to publish anything about other people which would tend 'to lower them in the eyes of right-thinking people'. You must not bring others into 'hatred, ridicule or contempt'.

To defame someone in writing or some other permanent form (including, incidentally, a statement made on radio or television) is a libel. To speak ill of another is slander.

The fact that a statement is true does not prevent it from being defamatory, but no one is entitled to a good name which he or she has not earned. So, if sued for a defamatory statement which you can prove to be true, you may plead 'justification'. You may claim that the statement was substantially true. The effect of a plea of justification is to repeat – and even more loudly and publicly – the very same defamatory statement that you made before. Hence if a plea of justification fails, your offence has been severely aggravated. The damages awarded against you will be greatly increased.

A much more helpful defence is 'qualified privilege'. The law recognizes that certain statements must be made for the public good. People must be entitled to speak their minds. Hence 'privilege'.

No action in defamation can succeed in respect of any statement made by anyone in a court of law. 'Absolute privilege' also applies to all statements made in Parliament. However malicious, untrue or unjustified a statement made in court or Parliament, it can never give rise to a successful defamation action.

Similar privilege attaches to occasions upon which the law recognizes that the writer of the statement has a public or private duty to make it and the reader a direct interest in receiving it. For instance, references are business necessities. So the givers of references are protected. They are under a moral duty to speak their minds to the inquirers (although, note, they have no legal duty to supply the reference). The recipient of the reference obviously has an interest in knowing its contents. The occasion is 'privileged'.

Or suppose that you have to write to a colleague about a possible sacking. Your letter alleges that the person was dishonest ... slovenly ... disobedient ... stupid ... unfit to be in your company. He or she is defamed. But clearly, this sort of letter *must* be written. It is essential company business. The occasion is 'privileged'.

But while privilege in courts and Parliament is 'absolute', when you write or speak to colleagues or supply references the privilege is 'qualified'. The qualification? If the statement was made out of 'malice', the privilege evaporates. 'Malice' simply means some wrongful motive. If it can be shown that the object of making the statement was to harm the person defamed rather than to assist the management in reaching a sensible conclusion, or the prospective employer in deciding whether or not to employ an applicant, the privilege goes. The law is not designed to shield the spiteful.

There is another defence for the writer of evil words: 'Fair comment on a matter of public interest.' So your words must be a statement of *opinion* and not of alleged *fact*. If they were partly opinion and partly fact, then insofar as they are fact, they must be substantially correct. Comment to your heart's content, but do no mis-state facts.

The comment must be 'fair'. This does not mean that the recipient or reader or the person referred to must consider it reasonable. In practice, this word exercises little restraint on your comment. Provided you are not simply using the occasion to forward a private grudge rather than to comment on a matter of public interest, you should have nothing to worry about. But do not confuse fact with fiction and, under the guise of comment, propagate false statements about your enemies.

Writers, then, should watch their words, whenever they are writing evil. Remember the three little monkeys? The one with his hands clapped firmly over his mouth is the most intelligent of all. Speak no evil and you need fear no action in slander.

As usual with the law this also applies in reverse. If you are at the receiving end of unkind words, apply these principles and you will know whether, in theory at least, you might have a good action in defamation against your defamer. Do not be surprised, though, if you are advised by your lawyer not to sue.

Defamation proceedings are perilous and unpredictable. Even if you win, you will endure worry, aggravation and expense.

The rich, the determined and the fortunate sometimes succeed, and are very handsomely recompensed for their risk by the jury's award. For instance, Jeffrey Archer, the novelist and former MP, was awarded £500,000 for an untrue newspaper story.

53

Sedition, injurious falsehood and other written traps

There are various other ways in which the law interferes with freedom of speech or writing. They are all rare in practice, but still require a weather eye from the letterwriter. So here is a miscellany of civil and criminal consequences which can arise out of use of the wrong word.

The offence of 'sedition' embraces all those practices, whether by word, writing or deed, which fall short of high treason but directly tend or have for their object to excite dissatisfaction or discontent ... to create public disturbance, or to lead to civil war ... to bring into hatred or contempt the sovereign or the government, the constitution or the laws of the realm ... to excite ill-will between different classes of the sovereign's subjects ... to incite people forcibly to obstruct the execution of the law ...' and so on, and so on.

In theory, this offence might put a heavy rein on free political discussion. But in practice it, too, is almost as dead as the proverbial dodo.

Only slightly less dormant is 'criminal libel' — which covers any defamatory publication which the publisher cannot show to be true *and* published in the public interest. This ancient offence has been said to be justified by the need to stop outraged gentlemen taking up their swords to avenge the attack on their reputation. Like the duel, it has largely slipped into history.

Not so perjury. If any person who is 'lawfully sworn as a witness or as an interpreter in a judicial proceeding wilfully makes a statement material in that proceeding which he (or she) knows to be false or does not believe to be true ...' he or she is a perjurer and may be imprisoned for up to seven years or fined an unlimited amount — or both. So when appearing before any 'tribunal, court of person having by law power to hear, examine and receive evidence on oath', mind what you say. And remember that written sworn evidence must be as accurate as you can make it (see Chapter 54 on Affidavits).

Although there are prosecutions for perjury, when you consider the number of perjurers it is obvious that the fear of committing this offence has about as little effect on the dishonest witness as the terror of purgatory.

Now for some civil results of uncivil words.

As we have seen in the last chapter, defamation may lead to trouble. But has it occurred to you that to speak ill of a person's *goods* may be defamatory of his person? Suppose, for instance, that you say: 'Jones is turning out really shoddy stuff these days and selling it at a very high price'. You are hardly heaping compliments on Jones — you are saying, in effect, 'That man Jones is a rogue — he is selling low-quality goods at a high price.'

Apart from libel and slander, words may themselves give 'a cause of action' if they cause damage to a person 'in the conduct of his affairs' or are calculated to cause him pecuniary loss.

Suppose, first, than any sort of property is up for sale. Someone 'without lawful motive' untruly writes that the property is charged, or that there are liabilities upon it, or that the vendor is not in a position to sell. This is 'slander of title'.

Again, if you write that someone is selling goods in infringement of copyright or patent, you may be committing 'slander of title'. But nowadays there are various statutory remedies available to people accused of this sort of behaviour (for instance, section 70 of the Patents Act 1977, which says that a person who is threatened with proceedings for infringement of the patent may bring an action for a declaration that the threats are unjustifiable, claim an injunction and, if any loss has been suffered, claim for damages.

Again, falsely and maliciously to disparage the quality of someone's goods may create a 'cause of action' — if the disparagement prevents their sale. By all means indulge in 'mere trade puffery', but 'knocking' may lead to trouble.

So where a false statement is made maliciously (out of a desire to injure and without lawful authority) and produces as its direct consequence 'damage which is capable of legal estimation', an action may lie for slander of title, slander of goods 'or other malicious falsehood'.

Finally, just a note on 'malice'. 'Maliciously' has been defined as meaning 'without just cause or excuse'. Unlawfully and intentionally to do 'without just excuse or occasion' an action which causes damage may lead to trouble. But it is certainly malicious to act out of some improper or dishonest motive or with the intention of causing injury. Where there is 'a distinct intention to injure the plaintiff apart from honest defence of the defendant's own property', an action may lie without there being any defamation as such. (For 'malice' as affecting the defence of 'qualified privilege', see chapter 52).

So, if you improperly or dishonestly attack the title or property or products of your competitors, they may have a good claim against you. The law approves of competition but frowns upon the more unpleasant forms of 'knocking' the goods and property of others.

54

Affidavits and oaths

An affidavit is a statement of fact, sworn by the 'deponent'. If on conscientious grounds the witness declines to take an oath, then he may make the appropriate declaration. What matters is that the court then has a document made by the witness, presumably as a result of careful thought and, if necessary, research. He is undertaking to tell the truth. If he lies, he is a perjurer.

Far too many affidavits are made far too carelessly. Suppose, for instance, that you want 'summary judgment'. You have issued a writ; there is no apparent defence (or 'triable issue') so your solicitors ask the court to give swift, sharp judgment, without the necessity of a trial. An affidavit will have to be filed, verifying the facts in the writ and saying that there is no defence (or no defence to that part of the claim in respect of which summary judgment is sought).

Affidavits may be sworn by solicitors. It is then for them to make sure that they are satisfied as to the truth of their assertion or as to the 'information and belief' to which they depose. But the solicitor may provide you with the draft document and ask you to take it to a Commissioner for Oaths and have it sworn.

Even if the solicitor has had the document handsomely and apparently permanently typed on special 'engrossing' paper, this should not deter you from perusing every word with care. After all, morality apart, the other side may not cave in; the case may reach trial; if it does, the odds are that you will have to give evidence. If you end up in the witness box, you will be cross-examined on the basis of your sworn affidavit. A mistake can be very expensive indeed. Take care what you say. Mind your words – particularly when they are written and sworn.

55

The effect of a signature

In business a handshake may no longer be an enforceable bond. But a signature still means much.

If you sign a letter put before you by your secretary or assistant or executive and (because you rely upon his or her honesty or skill or judgment) you sign without reading it, please do not think that you will afterwards be able to avoid the legal results of that letter, at least in so far as third parties are concerned. You will be bound by it. That is the major effect of the famous decision in the case of *Gallie* v. *Lee*.

Mrs Gallie was a lady in her eighties. She had a trusted nephew named Walter Parkin, who had been kind to her over the years. He was sole beneficiary under her will and a few years before she had decided to give him her house: 'Everything I possessed belongs to him', she said. He wanted to raise money on the house and she was willing for him to do so, provided that she could stay in it during her lifetime.

Unfortunately, Mr Parkin had a friend called Lee, who needed money to pay off *his* creditors. On the advice of a solicitor's managing clerk (who was later gaoled), Lee arranged for documents to be drawn up by which Mrs Gallie would sell the house to him for £3,000. Lee would not pay this, but he would mortgage the property.

Lee then prevailed upon Mrs Gallie to sign the document. Unfortunately, her glasses were either mislaid or broken and she did not read what she was signing. 'What is it for?', she asked Mr Lee. 'it is a deed of gift for Wally for the house,' Lee replied. She signed. Lee paid her nothing. The solicitors got him a £2,000 loan from the Anglia Building Society. Lee raised money on a second mortgage, but defaulted on the instalments. The building society sued for possession. Mrs Gallie and her nephew pleaded *non est factum* – that the document was not hers.

Mere mistakes in the contents of a document you sign will never allow you to avoid its effect. If you are aware of its essential nature, then it is yours, even if the contents are not as you think. However, if the document is entirely different in character and nature from that which you believed you were signing, you may be able to establish that it has no effect.

What, then, of Mrs Gallie's gift?

'A man who has failed to read a document and signs it should not be allowed to repudiate it as against an innocent purchaser,' said Lord Denning. 'His remedy is against the person who deceived him.' Even if he could plead fraud or mistake against the immediate party (that is, the person who induced the signature of the document), he would not be able to avoid the consequences 'when it had come into the hands of one who had in all innocence advanced money on the faith of it being his document, or had otherwise relied on it ...'

The principle? 'Whenever a man of full age and understanding who can read and write signs a legal document put before him for signature which on its face is intended to have legal consequences, then, if he does not take the trouble to read it but signs it as it is, relying on the word of another as to its character or effect or contents, he cannot be heard to say it is not his document.'

Lord Justice Russell agreed. Mrs Gallie, he said, had intended to sign a document divesting herself of her interest in the house. This she had done. Here was no case of *non est factum*. Lord Justice Salmon agreed. A court, he said, 'thus achieves a result which accords with reason and justice'.

So mind what you sign. And if people try to say that they did not realize what they were signing, then just refer them or their solicitors to the case of *Gallie* v. *Lee** and that should be the last you hear of that bad argument.

---

*The Court of Appeal's decision was affirmed by the House of Lords, where the case was known as *Saunders* v. *Anglia Building Society*.

56

Negligence – writing without due care

If someone else suffers damage as a result of a careless statement, it may lead to trouble all round. That was one effect of an important decision of the House of Lords.

A well-known merchant bank was asked for a reference. The inquirers wished to know whether a certain company was worthy of credit. The bank supplied the information; and when this turned out to be incorrect the inquirers lost their money. They sued the bank, claiming that although they (the inquirers) were not customers and the information was supplied gratuitously, the bank still 'owed them a duty of care' – that is, was under a duty to them to exercise such care as was reasonable in all the circumstances to ensure that the information given was correct.

'Nonsense,' retorted the bank. 'We supplied the service at no charge and you cannot expect us to have the same liability to you as we would have had if you had been a customer or we had charged you. And anyway,' they added, 'there was a disclaimer on the reference saying that it was given "without responsibility" on the part of the bank or its officers.' And they denied negligence.

The trial judge held that they had been negligent. They were under a duty of care, even though the service was given gratuitously. This decision was eventually upheld by the House of Lords, but that the effect of the disclaimer was to let them off the hook.

The basic principle was established long ago. We each owe a duty of care to our 'neighbour'. A 'neighbour', in this sense, is any person who we ought reasonably to anticipate would be likely to be affected by our negligent act. If, then, you are a manufacturer, you have a liability in contract to the people who buy your goods. If the goods are faulty, then you are in breach of contract. If you are negligent and they suffer injury, loss or damage, then you may be held liable.

But your responsibility does not end there. It extends to 'the ultimate consumer'. Suppose that you manufacture drink. It must be obvious to you that the person who is likely to drink it is not the wholesaler or retailer to whom you actually sell the stuff. The 'ultimate consumer' – the customer of the retailer or caterer – is the person who will be poisoned if the drink is defective. He or she is the 'neighbour' of the manufacturer.

So there is a liability in the law of negligence not only to those whom you know but even to complete strangers.

'The bank', said the House of Lords, in effect, 'must be taken to have realized that the reference was asked for with a purpose in mind. The intention was that the reference be acted upon. So the bank ought to have realized that if the reference was incorrect, the result might well be that the recipient would suffer damage. So the bank owed a duty of care to that recipient, even though the service was given gratuitously.' The milk of human kindness may prove a very costly commodity.

So negligence had been found against the bank and a duty of care was owed. The damage was also proved. That left the disclaimer. The bank had given the reference upon the explicit and clear understanding that it was not to be held responsible for the accuracy of the document. The recipient could not go behind that disclaimer, which was fully effective in protecting the bank. As a result, the House of Lords did not have to consider the question of whether the defendants had been guilty of negligence. The bank escaped because of its disclaimer.

Since that decision*, many business people have shivered slightly and taken insurance cover. The giver of every sort of reference must take care not only to avoid defamation in circumstances in which malice may be imputed to them (see Chapter 52), but must also be careful to ensure that, if asked for a reference for one Peter Smith, they do not provide it in respect of another. They owe a 'duty of care' to the recipient – and to Peter Smith.

The case of John Lawton† demonstrates this point. After he was made redundant, Mr Lawton used his former employer's name when he applied for a new job. They took up his references with a form of questionnaire, which was duly answered; and his new employers immediately dismissed him because the answers were so unfavourable. Somehow Mr Lawton got hold of a copy of the reference. He felt it was so inaccurate that it showed 'culpable negligence' by the personnel manager; so he sued.

'Even if we were negligent,' replied the firm, 'and even if we were liable to the new employers, we cannot be made liable to the man himself.' But the court disagreed: 'There is ... no doubt that the plaintiff relied upon the defendants to give an accurate opinion and state accurate facts in the reference'.

Unfortunately for John Lawton, the court also found that there was no negligence, because there was enough evidence for his ex-employers to have reached their unhappy conclusions about him.

Not only employers writing references need to take care. What you write – or even what you say – when trying to persuade people to work for you may be quoted against you in court. Mr McNally‡ applied for a job at an oil refinery in Libya. He was interviewed by Mr James, on behalf of the firm. Mr James gave him a number of assurances about the job. Mr McNally signed a contract. The small print said that if he did not pass various tests, his employment could be terminated. In the event, he lasted ten days in Libya before being dismissed with (eventually) wages in lieu of notice. The job was not one for which he was in any way qualified.

Not content to sue the firm for leading him thousands of miles under false pretences, Mr McNally sued Mr James for negligently misrepresenting what was on offer. He won substantial damages. Despite the defendant's argument that there was no more than 'a moral duty to protect the ambitious employee from himself', the judge ruled: 'The questions here are whether Mr James took it upon himself to advise the plaintiff whether he was qualified for the job, and whether as a result of that advice the plaintiff was induced to enter into the contract.' The answer to both questions was 'yes'.

It is not enough to prove that you were negligent in giving the advice or information concerned. To obtain damages against you, your correspondents – like Mr McNally – would have to prove two other things: first, that the statement concerned was acted upon; second, that they suffered damage, foreseeably arising from the negligence.

Infallibility being a divine attribute, everyone in business makes mistakes. Happily, most of them lead nowhere too disastrous. Indeed the great advantage of making a mistake is that next time you may recognize it. If others do the recognizing, then that is unfortunate. But it is only if they do not realize that you have been in error and actually take action as a result of your mistake that they will have a legal remedy.

Suppose, for instance that you make a misleading statement in a letter. As a result, the recipient consults his board, his solicitor, his accountant, his management consultant and then – bolstered by expert approval – takes action along the lines you have suggested. The chances are that he could not blame you. There were too many intervening people, facts and ideas.

Alternatively, suppose you make some provocative statement. It may never enter your mind that anyone would be stupid enough to act upon it without further research or inquiry. But may be you were being obtuse. The question is: would the 'reasonable person' have expected you to have foreseen that your correspondent would act upon your words? Should you reasonably have prophesied, had you applied your mind to the situation, that your words would give rise to someone else's action? If not, then your mistake will lead nowhere – at least so far as you are concerned.

Assume, now, that the recipient of your letter can overcome both these hurdles. He has still not reached the end of the trail. He must show that the damage was not 'too remote'. Take an example from an ordinary road traffic accident. Your employee caused it through careless driving? You are responsible, as if you yourself had been at the wheel, if the man was driving in the course of his employment. Therefore you would have to compensate anyone who suffered injury, loss or damage as a reuslt – provided that this was foreseeable.

So the cost of repairing the other vehicle, or reimbursing the injured man for his lost wages, or damages in respect of his personal injuries – all these can be laid at your door.

But suppose, on the other hand, that the other driver missed an important appointment and hence a potentially profitable contract. That would be his misfortune. That damage would be 'too remote'.

All this involes some very complicated legal considerations. If your letterwriting leads to the threat of legal action, the sooner you get to your solicitor, the better. Meanwhile, treat this chapter as a warning – and take care.

---

* *Hedley Byrne* v. *Heller and Partners* (1964).
† *Lawton* v. *B.O.C. Transhield Ltd.*
‡ *McNally* v. *Welltrade International Ltd.*

57

Letters at work

Of course you do business on paper. You cannot write all your own letters, all of the time, can you? Even if you insist on signing all your own mail, this chore probably comes at the end of the day, when your mind is weary and your soul longing for hearth or home, bed or bottle. You make mistakes.

Or are you a chauffeur-driven executive, signing mail in the back of the car? Then what if the driver lets his mind wander and negligently causes a collision?

Whether the employee's mistake is made in words or on wheels, the employer may not be the only sufferer. But who will be liable to pay? Consider the legal rules on 'vicarious liability' – when the sins of the employee may be laid at the door of the employer.

Every employer is liable to third parties in respect of damage caused by employees within the scope of their employment. If you have the benefit of someone's work, then you must accept the burden of his or her mistakes. On the other hand, the mere fact that you employ people does not mean that they are bound to you, every long hour of the day. They are free to sail off on independent frolics of their own. When they do so improperly, they are outside the scope of their employment and their employers bear no responsibility for their misdeeds.

Your secretary may operate a typing bureau from her home. If she does so on her own account and in her own time, then she is responsible for her own negligence. You normally bear no liability.

Or maybe your driver crashes a car while off on an evening's gambol. The fact that he happens to be in the company car will not place liability on the company.

Was the negligent employee acting 'within the course of his employment', or was he 'independently frolicking?'

An attendant at a petrol station was forbidden to smoke. He lit a cigarette and threw down the match. The devastating explosion destroyed property belonging to third parties.

'He was not employed to smoke,' argued his employers. 'Indeed, he was forbidden to do so.'

'He was employed to put petrol into tanks,' said the court. 'At the time of the accident, that is precisely what he was doing – although in a thoroughly negligent, improper and forbidden way.' His employers were liable.

So the test is *not*: 'Was the employee doing something forbidden?', but rather: 'Was he or she about the employer's business?' Tell your employees what not to do and (if their misbehaviour is sufficiently serious) you may dismiss them if they disobey. But for third parties, what matters is whether or not the employees were doing their job.

Suppose, then, that your secretary is guilty of a clerical error. Perhaps he or she leaves a nought off the price of goods offered. At the foot of the document we read: 'Dictated by Mr Smith but signed in his absence'. Poor unfortunate Mr Smith – he should have been there. The company will be bound by the offer just as it would have been if Mr Smith had signed it himself – or, for that matter, if it had carried the company seal.

You are asked for a reference. You hand it over to your personnel manager for attention. Negligently, she provides the wrong information – and in breach of your instructions she omits to include a disclaimer of liability? The recipient of the missive suffers damage through relying upon the carelessly written words? Then it will be no answer to the claim to say: My employee was guilty, not I'. Her carelessness, committed in the course of her employment by you, is your own. In some ways, husband and wife are still regarded as one by the law – but employer and employee are united far more often when it comes to the rules on vicarious liability.

A letter arrives at the office, shop or factory. It is addressed to a member of staff, care of the firm. You open it. It contains confidential information. 'Anything that comes to the firm is liable to be opened,' you say. But are you right?

If the letter is addressed to James Smith, c/o Jones Ltd, then Mr Smith must expect to have it opened. The normal procedure in most businesses is for the mail to be opened centrally and then passed out to the appropriate departments or individuals for attention.

If an envelope is marked 'Personal' or 'Confidential', then the employer has no right to open it. Instead of coming to the employee in the course of his or her employment, it has simply arrived at the place of employment. To open it then would be to interfere with Her Majesty's mail. And if by mistake you open a letter not intended for you and discover its highly confidential contents, the law says you may not make use of, or pass on, those confidences.

Unhappily, the post is sometimes used for vicious purposes. These include the sending of letter and parcel bombs; of 'poison-pen' letters; and of pornographic literature.

Members of parliament and others in public life who are vulnerable to the cowardly evil of letter bombs should take specific advice from appropriate police or security officials. Some organisations screen mail. But individuals at risk should not only themselves watch their mail with an eagle and a suspicious eye but they should instruct, reinstruct and remind their staff to do the same. The security people will tell you what to look out for and how. But if any letter or package appears suspicious, do not move it. Call the police.

58

Contracts

A contract is a bargain made between two or more people. It has a number of essential elements. First, there must be an unconditional offer. Second, this offer must be unconditionally accepted. Third, there must be 'consideration'. Fourth, the required formalities of the law must be complied with – and writing may be one of these. Let us start with the writing.

Generally, no formalities are required for a contract to be binding. Most contracts are as complete and binding in law if they are made orally as if every term were written in letters of gold. There are exceptions: contracts of guarantee or for the transfer of an interest in land must be evidenced by some sufficient note or memorandum in writing, signed by the party to be charged. Contracts of hire purchase, of marine or life insurance and for the transfer of shares require writing; so does a contract of apprenticeship. But a contract to buy goods may be made orally, so a telephone conversation is sufficient to wrap up the deal. So, too, a contract of employment (but see next chapter).

Where a deal has not been made or confirmed in writing, it may be difficult to prove its terms. One party may say that one term was agreed, the other something different.

So do confirm your agreements in writing whenever you can. And do make a note or confirm anything important said to you on the telephone. Remember, if a dispute follows and reaches court, you will be allowed to refer in the witness box to notes made at the time.

What about the other essentials? First, the offer. 'I offer to sell you X quantity of Y brand goods.' That is an offer. Simple? Not necessarily. It is, for instance, important to distinguish an offer from a mere 'invitation to treat'. If you advertise goods, you will not necessarily be bound to sell them, either at the advertised price or at all. Basically, the position is the same as when goods are on display in a shop window. They are not 'offered for sale', in the technical, legal sense. Potential buyers are invited to make offer to buy. Those offers may be either accepted or refused; or a counter-offer may be made – that is, an offer on different terms.

Second, the offer must be *unconditional*. If you say, 'I'll sell you these goods, provided that I've enough in stock,' you can get out of the deal if you have not enough in stock. It is not an offer capable of immediate acceptance.

Third, *unconditional* acceptance: the offer must be accepted in its entirety. For instance, suppose that you offer to buy goods which your see advertised. You set out the price you are prepared to pay and the dates when you wish to have delivery and you leave no 'ifs' or 'buts'. The supplier writes back saying: 'Thank you for your letter. Your order is hereby accepted and we confirm that delivery will be made in accordance therewith.' The deal is done.

Now suppose the letter of acceptance contains, printed at the bottom or on the back, terms and conditions inconsistent with your own. In effect, the suppliers are saying: 'We accept your offer – but subject to your agreeing to our terms and conditions as printed hereon'. This is not an *unconditional* acceptance. It is a 'counter-offer' which may be accepted or rejected by potential buyers as they see fit.

Once you realize this, you tend to take a closer look at the terms and conditions on letters or other documents of this kind. Remember that if you do nothing about them and simply accept the goods, the chances are that the counter-offer will be the offer and your acceptance of the goods will be the acceptance. Hence, that acceptance will be subject to the supplier's terms and conditions. An exception to this is exclusion clauses, which may not be valid if they are unreasonable.

But what if the buyer never reads one of the terms in tiny type? Too bad. Provided that it is legible and not excluded by law, it is still one of the terms of the contract. If people do not choose to read contractual documents that is their look-out.

What if they couldn't have understood the terms, even if they had read them? Then they should have asked a lawyer to explain them. Only customers under the age of eighteen or of unsound mind may be able to avoid their contractual obligations.

Generally, the terms of the contract, whether oral or written, are part of the bargain. If that bargain is binding, those terms will be included in it, provided only that these were sufficiently brought to the attention of the contracting parties. (Like the words on the back of a ticket, referring you to the company's regulations.)

Like an offer, an acceptance (if it is to conclude the bargain) must be unconditional. If, for instance, the buyer says, 'I accept your offer of these goods, subject to approval by my directors,' then there is no deal until the directors have given their approval and this fact has been communicated to the supplier.

Now comes the fourth essential: 'Consideration'. This, in English law, simply means some *quid pro quo* – some return for the value or promise given. 'In consideration of our paying you £..., you agree to supply me with ....' The consideration 'moving' in one direction is the promise to pay the specified sum; in the other direction, it is the promise to supply the goods in return for that sum.

'The customer should have put down a deposit, I suppose ...'. Correct. He or she would then have been saying, 'In consideration of my giving you this deposit, you agree to hold the goods at our disposal for the specified period'. If you had accepted the money, you would have been bound to give the customer the option on the goods concerned for the period agreed.

Conversely, (the deposit being an 'earnest of good faith' on the customer's part), if he or she had failed to exercise the option and to take up the goods, you would have been entitled to keep the deposit. As usual, you *could* have made some agreement to the contrary. You could, for instance, have agreed to give credit in the same sum as the deposit, if your customer decided to opt not to purchase ...

If a buyer allows one of his servants to place an order on his behalf, then he is as bound by that order as if he had given it himself. This must be so or the business world would halt. A company has no existence in human form. Someone must act for it. Even individuals cannot do everything for themselves. If you give someone your authority to contract on your behalf, then you will not be able to avoid the contracts made by that person pursuant to that authority.

'But suppose that the person had no authority ... can the principal then refuse to accept the arrangement made?' That depends. He can do so if the agent had neither his actual nor his 'apparent' authority. Otherwise he is almost certainly bound.

If you 'hold someone out' as having your authority to act on your behalf (if, in legal terms, you give them your 'ostensible' authority) then you are, in effect, saying to other people: 'This person is my agent, entitled to contract on my behalf'. If someone relies upon this statement and as a result makes a bargain with you, then you will be bound by that bargain. You must not 'hold out' people as having authority which they do not in fact possess. If you do, you cannot expect the law to free you from deals made as a result.

Finally, the contract must not be 'too vague to be enforceable'. The law will not make contracts for business people who do not bother to do so for themselves. So sometimes it is possible to avoid a contract if it can be shown that any of the essential elements of that contract are missing.

For example, suppose that your customers had agreed to buy goods. The delivery date was fixed and the goods themselves were decided upon. But you left the price unfixed. Alternatively, suppose that the price was fixed but that the quantity to be taken was not. In either case, one of the essential terms of the deal was missing. The contract would be too vague to be enforced.

To sum up: if a person of full capacity makes an unconditional offer which is unconditionally accepted by some other person of full capacity and the terms of the contract are adequately set out and agreed between them – and provided that there is 'consideration' – the contract is complete. Where an agent makes the contract on behalf of his principal, it rarely matters whether that agent had the actual authority of the principal to contract on his behalf. It is enough if the agent had his principal's apparent authority to do so. And writing is only necessary in exceptional cases. When required, it should always be undertaken with precision and care.

59

Contracts of employment

A contract of employment is an agreement between employer and employee under which the employee agrees to serve and the employer to employ, on the terms stated. A contract of employment (with the sole exception of a contract of apprenticeship) does not have to be in writing to be fully binding in law. But thanks to the Employment Protection (Consolidation) Act 1978, the employee must be given written particulars of its most important terms within thirteen weeks of the start of employment or within four weeks of any variation.

The written statement, which may be contained in one or more letters or other documents, must identify the parties (especially important if the employer is a company which is part of a group). It must specify the date when the employment began and state whether or not the employment is continuous with any previous employment (if so, then when did that employment begin?). It must state the employee's job title. And it must give the following particulars of the terms of employment as at a specified date not more than one week before the statement is given:

1 The scale or rate of remuneration, or the method of calculating remuneration.
2 The intervals at which remuneration is paid (that is, whether weekly or monthly or by some other period).
3 Any terms and conditions relating to hours of work (including any terms and conditions relating to normal working hours).
4 Any terms and conditions relating to:
   a Holidays and holiday pay (including the manner in which holiday entitlement is arrived at, especially when the employment comes to an end).
   b Incapacity for work due to sickness or injury, including any

provisions for sick pay.
c Pensions and pension schemes.
5 The length of notice which the employee is obliged to give and entitled to receive to determine the contract of employment.
6 To whom the employee may turn if he or she has a grievance or a query regarding disciplinary procedures – plus details of both grievance and disciplinary procedures or where these may easily be found.

The particulars need not be in any set form and may (and generally should) include other terms not required by law, such as:
a Clauses giving employers the right to search employees or their property.
b Restraint clauses.
c Clauses warning employees that breaches of the employer's health and safety rules may lead to dismissal.

Employees are (generally, and in broad terms) only entitled by law to written particulars when they have been employed for thirteen weeks. Any changes must be notified within four weeks. As for unfair dismissal protection and redundancy pay, to qualify for written particulars employees must work at least sixteen hours a week, or eight hours after five years' continuous service.

If the particulars given are disputed, an industrial tribunal has the power to decide who is right, and to 'declare' the correct particulars. Remember, the contract is made when you offer employment and the candidate accepts. Issuing particulars is not an opportunity to rewrite the contract.

So the prudent employer makes all employment offers in writing, with a reference in the letter to the detailed particulars. These may be in the form of a works handbook, or a collective agreement with a trade union.

It is worth your time and effort to get employment contracts correct, because disputes can be very costly and time-consuming. Bear in mind that you cannot unilaterally, without every employee's consent, change what is in their contracts – short of dismissal, offering new jobs all round, and running the risk of a claim for damages for unfair dismissal.

60

Letters in dispute

The more serious or costly the dispute, the more vital the correspondence is likely to prove, and the more weighty its probative value. So the courts have evolved a system to ensure that most correspondence, material to an action, is revealed to the other side (if they do not already possess it), and produced for the court's inspection. This process is called 'discovery of documents'.

In any legal action, the parties must set out their contentions in so-called 'pleadings'. In the High Court (which deals, in general, with claims over £5,000), the plaintiff's 'cause of action' is pleaded in a 'Statement of Claim'.

Next, the defendant puts his or her answer into a 'Defence'. This may include a 'Counterclaim'. The plaintiff will then file his or her 'Reply' and 'Defence to Counterclaim'.

In the County Court, an action starts with a 'Particulars of Claim'; and this is succeeded by a Defence (with or without Counterclaim) and a Reply.

If any of the 'pleadings' is obscure or does not set out the case in sufficient detail, 'Further and Better Particulars' may be sought by the other party. If the litigant has not declared his or her case adequately, there will now be a chance to do so, if necessary as a result of a court order.

The object of the exercise, then, is to enable trial judges to have the contentions of both sides spread out before them, so that (on the basis of the evidence, and the law) they may decide the matter one way or the other.

If any document is referred to in a pleading, the other parties are entitled to a copy of it. If, for instance, your claim rests on a letter or an invoice, or on written particulars of a contract of employment, the other parties may demand a copy and on payment of the appropriate copying charges (if any) are entitled to have one.

Moreover, where a pleading does not specifically rely on a document, but there may be some relevant letter, plan, map, order form or what-have-you, upon which the party intends to rely, the other litigant may demand that the document be 'identified'.

Once the 'pleadings are closed', and the contentions of the parties are clearly set out on paper, the time has come for each to reveal documents relevant to the proceedings, which are or have been in their possession. 'Discovery' will take place of all material documents, and these must then be made available for 'inspection'. Litigants are not allowed to keep some useful document up their sleeve, only to produce it with a flourish at the hearing, preferably while cross-examining a star witness on the other side. They must reveal it beforehand.

To make sure this is done, a formal list of documents has to be prepared and presented. Sometimes, the list will be supported by affidavits in which the litigant swears that these are all the relevant documents which are or have been in his or her possession.

Sometimes, instead of a list, the documents will be set out as part of an affidavit. Not all relevant documents must be shown. Some are 'privileged'. For instance, any correspondence which you may have with your own solicitor will be privileged. Nor must you produce an Advice given to you by your own lawyer. But letters which passed between the parties and which were not written 'without prejudice' (next chapter) will have to be revealed, even if they go against your case.

So that explains why the art of letterwriting is such an important adjunct to successful litigation. Careless letters cost cases. So mind how you write. Your letter may one day be read out in court. Better still, it may win your case before it reaches trial, which, of course, is by far the best sort of legal victory.

Parliament has recently added to the legal protection given to victims of poison-pen letters – and of unjustified or malicious threats such as are sometimes used by the unscrupulous to intimidate their debtors. Such letters are now sent at peril of prosecution.

Your natural reaction may be, 'Good, about time too, but nothing for me to worry about.' But the law is widely, and a little vaguely, drawn, and you *do* need to bear in mind the limits on what you can put in a letter without risking the recipient being able to take the matter to the police. This is what the new law – the Malicious Communications Act 1988 – prohibits:

- sending letters or articles which convey an indecent or grossly offensive message
- sending threatening letters
- including deliberately false information in a letter
- sending anything else which is of an indecent or grossly offensive nature

In each of these situations, an offence is only committed if the sender intended to cause distress or anxiety to the recipient. And it is a defence to show that a threat, if that is the source of the complaint, was used to reinforce a claim which the sender believed he or she had reasonable grounds to make, and the sender believed the threat was a reasonable way of pursuing the claim. So a threat of court action if your debtor does not pay up may be acceptable. But it will not be so if you do not honestly believe in the validity of your claim. Nor will it be reasonable even for genuine claims to peddle false information to distress your debtors into paying.

Consumers' representatives are waking up to the possible use of the new law to control some undesirable debt-collecting methods: make sure you are not open to legal attack.

61

'Without prejudice'

What is the effect of putting 'without prejudice' at the top of your letters? If you enter into negotiations which (as they inevitably will) involve concessions on your part, can these be thrown back in your face if the negotiations fail and the case gets to court? How far is it safe to make admissions in correspondence if you put the magic words 'without prejudice' at the top of the letter?

The answers were given in the notable case of *Tomlin* v. *Standard Telephones & Cables Ltd*. Mr Tomlin was injured at work and sued his employers. Negotiations followed between his solicitors and his employers' insurers. Eventually, the insurers made an offer which was refused. Mr Tomlin pressed forward with his action. He also alleged that an agreement had been arrived at during the negotiations that he was entitled to be compensated on the basis that he and his employers were each fifty per cent responsible for the accident. The *amount* of damages was not agreed.

Was the correspondence between the parties admissible? All the letters that mattered had been marked 'without prejudice'. Eventually, by a majority of two to one, the Court of Appeal decided that, in the circumstances, the letters could be looked at by the court.

The effect of 'without prejudice' letters was laid down by a judge, many years ago. He said this: 'I think they mean "without prejudice" to the position of the writer of the letter if the terms he proposes *are not* accepted. If the terms proposed in the letter are accepted a complete contract is established, and the letter, although written "without prejudice", operates to alter the old state of things and to establish a new one.'

So, 'not only is the court entitled to look at the letters in this case,' said Lord Justice Danckwerts, but 'although they were described as "without prejudice", it is quite possible (and, in fact, the intention of the parties was) that there was a binding agreement contained in their correspondence.'

In other words, once 'without prejudice' negotiations have reached fruition, the court must be entitled to look at the letters to see whether that allegation is well founded. As Sir Gordon Willmer put it: 'It is no objection that the agreement is contained in letters which are headed "without prejudice".' If you make an agreement, then you cannot say: 'It was only made in the course of negotiations.' If the negotiations had failed, then the court would be entitled to know that there were in fact attempts at settlement, but the letters themselves would remain privileged. Once an agreement is reached, the court must be entitled to look at the letters in which it is contained. If the parties cannot agree as to whether or not the letters contained a binding agreement, the court must examine them if it is to decide.

Mr Justice Ormrod dissented. He said, 'The court will protect, and ought to protect so far as it can, in the public interest, "Without prejudice" negotiations because they are very helpful to the disposal of claims without the necessity for litigating in court. Therefore, nothing should be done to make more difficult or more hazardous negotiations under the umbrella of "without prejudice".

'I am well aware that letters get headed "without prejudice" in the most absurd circumstances, but the letters in the present case are not so headed unnecessarily or meaninglessly. They are plainly "without prejudice" letters. Therefore the Court should be very slow to lift the umbrella of "without prejudice" unless the case is absolutely plain.'

The judge looked at the correspondence, but decided that the case was not 'absolutely plain'.

Anyway, the principle is now clear enough. Mark your letters 'without prejudice', so as to ensure that if no agreement is reached your position will not be prejudiced through any admissions or confessions that you may have made. Once an agreement results from the negotiations, they cease to be 'without prejudice'. They are 'open', for all the world to see.

Another case when letters (but not their contents) may be considered is where there is unreasonable delay. In many cases plaintiffs have been driven out of court because they did not pursue their claims with sufficient vigour. On the other hand, it would be wrong for claims to be dismissed through delay where the parties were trying to avoid court battle through 'without prejudice' parleys.

So allow or encourage your solicitors to haggle. But if they delay when negotiations have ceased, then harry them.

Still, the actual contents of 'without prejudice' letters are only admissible where an offer contained in them has been accepted. So a court will not be allowed to see them merely where they contain admissions or acknowledgments of a debt, where it is alleged that the debt has become 'statute barred'. If the six-year period has passed since the debt was incurred or acknowledged in writing, the fact that there were intervening negotiations will not revive it.

If you want to keep your rights to your leased business premises, under the Landlord and Tenant Act 1954 (as amended) you must serve your notices and if necessary make application to the court within the period specified. If you are kept haggling until that date has passed, your rights will be lost. Whether the negotiations were oral or in writing, provided that they were 'without prejudice', your landlord's position will remain unaffected – unless, of course, you can prove you actually reached an agreement.

The privilege which the law gives to 'without prejudice' letters may be 'waived' by consent of the parties to the negotiations. If all agree that the court ought to see the letters, then so be it. If the writers of the letters wish to waive the privilege, some think that they can do so.

But most lawyers believe that unless both parties consent, or the letters reveal an agreement binding them in law, neither side can improve (or worsen) its position by throwing off the cloak of 'without prejudice' to reveal the contents of their correspondence.

So while Tomlin's case shows the limits of the doctrine, the basic principle remains unaffected. Put your negotiations under the umbrella of 'without prejudice' letters, and if agreement escapes you the chances are that the letters will remain hidden from the judicial eye, now and for ever more.

62

Proof of posting

'We never received your letter', you write.

'Too bad', answers your supplier (or customer or other correspondent). 'We can prove that we posted it; you will be presumed by law to have received it; so the offer you orginally made was validly accepted by us – and you had no right to sell the goods elsewhere.'

'Rubbish', you reply. But are you right? Anyway, how could your correspondent prove that he or she did post the letter? If a contract is made by post is it firm and binding when a letter of acceptance is posted or when it is received? At what stage can you (or your correspondent) still cry off?

Where a contract is entered into wholly or partly by correspondence, and where an offer is made by letter, the deal is done as soon as a 'properly addressed letter containing the acceptance is posted'. Provided that the 'offeree' accepts unconditionally and within the time specified in the correspondence, the 'offeror' cannot clamber out of his or her obligations by alleging that he never received the letter.

So proof of posting becomes important. Ideally the sender will have taken the trouble to get a receipt for the letter. Recorded delivery will show despatch and delivery and so will registered post.

But the vast majority of commercial correspondence is posted in the ordinary way, without any sort of post office record. Your office should have a posting book, in which the addressee of each letter is noted. Production of the book is not absolute proof, but there will be a presumption of posting which the addressee will find hard to rebut.

'The posting of a letter', says the law, 'may be proved by the person who posted it, or by showing facts from which posting may be presumed.' Hence 'evidence of posting may be given by proving that a letter was delivered to a clerk who in the ordinary course of business would have posted it.' Alternatively, it could be shown that the letter was put into a box which is normally cleared by the postman.

Again, if a letter is properly dated, that date will be taken as evidence of the date upon which is was written or dictated. In fact, evidence may show that dictation occurred a day or more before. The postmark on the envelope is good evidence of the time and place of posting.

So work out a sensible system for the recording of letters posted. And because these rules apply both ways, the stamping of a date or receipt on all incoming post is a very sensible precaution.

Note:
The rules are rather different where acceptance of an offer is by telex. Two cases, the more recent one in the House of Lords – *Brinkibon* v. *Stahag* (1982) – have established that the same general rule applicable to instantaneous communication also applies to telex.

Where an offer is accepted by telex, the time of acceptance is when the telex is sent and the place of acceptance will normally be where the telex is received and read and not (as in the case of a letter) the place from which it is sent.

Another increasingly important medium of commerce is the fax. As yet the courts have not been called on to decide whether telex rules will apply to fax. In a simple world the answer would be yes – but fax has one disadvantage over telex, that there is no proof your fax has arrived complete and in good order, with all pages fully transmitted. This may lead the courts to treat fax as no more than a very fast equivalent of the postal service.

Part 8

APPENDICES

'That will be the last letter for today Miss Wilkins . . . .'

1

Post Office services

Introduction

You may, of course, send your letter or card by hand. But the odds are that (for better or worse) you will use the services provided by the Post Office. And that use could be a great deal better, if you knew more about it.

Here, then, is a summary of the services offered by the Post Office (with my thanks to them for their co-operation). The descriptions are of necessity brief, and you are advised to consult the *Post Office Guide* for full details. You may regard some of the items as a checklist, worth a few moments of your time to ensure that you are making the best of the services which you know to exist. But you will also find some lesser-known services which may well save you a good deal of time, aggravation, worry – and expense – and hence contribute towards the commercial success of your letterwriting.

Letters

The system of first- and second-class postal services for inland letters is well established and all business people are familiar with it. We do not include details of rates for letters here since these have been more or less regularly increased and remain liable to change. Two points are, however, worth noting here. First, inland rates apply to letters from the UK to the Isle of Man, and the Channel Islands. Second, the maximum admissible weight for a second-class letter is 750 g – so really heavy letters are often sent much more economically – by parcel post.

Discounts on postage for pre-sorted first class letters

First class letter contracts: A service for posters mailing 4,000 or more first-class letters at any one time, pre-sorted into post towns (or equivalent postcodes). This pre-sorting attracts a ten per cent discount, rising to twelve per cent on fully postcoded mailings. An additional one per cent discount is given for postings before 1pm. Normal first-class delivery is given to these postings provided they meet the latest recommended posting times.

Discounts on postage for pre-sorted second class letters

Second class discount service: A service for posters mailing 4,000 or more second-class letters at any one time, pre-sorted into post towns and counties (or equivalent postcodes). Items pre-sorted to post towns attract a ten per cent discount and those pre-sorted into counties attract a five per cent discount. In both cases the discount is increased by two per cent for fully postcoded mailings. Normal second-class delivery is given.

Bulk rebate service

Bulk mailings of second-class letters pre-sorted into post towns or counties (or equivalent postcodes) which are not time critical can attract higher discounts, as shown below. Delivery will normally be within seven working days after posting (excluding weekends, bank and public holidays). Postage is pre-paid at second-class letter rates and a rebate is given after the letters have been posted and checked.

Number of letters	Amount of rebate
4,000 (minimum)-4,999	Postage paid on all letters in excess of 4,000
5,000-23,529	15% of the postage paid on all letters
23,530-24,999	Postage paid on all letters in excess of 20,000
25,000-96,875	20% of the postage paid on all letters
96,876-99,999	Postage paid on all letters in excess of 77,500
100,000-241,935	$22^1/2$% of the postage paid on all letters
241,936-249,999	Postage paid on all letters in excess of 187,500
250,000-933,333	25% of the postage paid on all letters
933,334-999,999	Postage paid on all letters in excess of 700,000
One million or more	30% of the postage paid on all letters

For all three services, items must normally be identical in shape, size and weight and no discount is given for items which are not pre-sorted.

Discounts are not available for bulk postings from the UK to the Channel Islands or the Isle of Man.

Mailsort

During 1989, these existing discount services will be replaced by Mailsort, a new streamlined service for businesses and other organizations sending pre-sorted mail. The existing delivery options will continue under Mailsort and posters will still attract discounts for pre-sorting their mail, but the terms and conditions for the three services will be simplified and the method of sorting will be based on the postcode.

More details about Mailsort can be obtained from your local Postal Sales Representative.

The Postcode Project

The Post Office can give free advice to help businesses postcode their mailing list. In addition, companies with computer held mailing lists may be eligible for a cash contribution to the cost of postcoding their lists. Further details are available from local Postal Sales Representatives.

Price protection

Direct mail deposit system. A contractual facility for direct mail advertisers. An advertiser who wishes to protect a mailing against the possibility of a postal tariff change occurring before the posting date planned for that mailing may do so by depositing with the Post Office 25 per cent of the postage due on that mailing, calculated at the rates current at the time the deposit is lodged. The deposit may be made up to six months in advance of the mailing date.

A mailing to be protected must be of at least 5,000 identical items containing advertising material only, and full details of the size, nature and timing of the mailing will be required. (A Direct Mail Deposit may not be used to protect a mailing against a proposed tariff increase that has already, at the time the deposit is lodged, been the subject of a public announcement by the Post Office.)

Door-to-door distribution of unaddressed leaflets

The household delivery service. This servce provides for the delivery of unaddressed material on a door-to-door basis in any area ranging from a single postcode sector to complete national coverage. No stamps are required and items may be enveloped or unenveloped provided they meet the following conditions:-

Minimum size	:	100mm × 70mm
Maximum size	:	300mm f 165mm (larger items can be delivered by arrangement)
Maximum thickness	:	17mm
Maximum weight	:	60g

All items in a distribution must be identical and bear the name and address of the sender. Delivery will normally be completed within two weeks of an agreed starting date, apart from December when the service is not generally available. Bulk supplies of items are, however, required one week in advance of the agreed starting date.

Prices vary according to the weight of the items involved and the total volume of the distribution. An additional charge for folding is also made for the delivery of items which exceed the maximum dimensions. Full details can be obtained from the Household Delivery Service National Booking Centre on 01-239 6777.

Reply services

Business Reply, Freepost and Admail are designed to encourage response to advertising or speedy payment of bills. Business Reply and Freepost are both ways of paying postage on behalf of the sender.

Business Reply pre-printed envelopes or cards are available for either first- or second-class post.

Freepost is a more flexible reply-paid service which can be used when pre-printed envelopes or cards cannot. Freepost addresses are short and easy to remember and can be quoted on advertising and sales literature, in press advertisements, TV or radio commercials and billboards. There is normally a small handling charge on top of postage for each reply received. Large users can claim discounts on the handling charge.

Business Reply and Freepost letters are normally delivered second post. There is a small extra charge for priority delivery.

Admail is a redirection service which enables advertisers to quote a prestigious or local address and have replies re-routed to a fulfilment house anywhere in the UK.

Compensation, registration and recorded delivery

The ordinary letter services are not designed as compensation services, but limited compensation – less than £25 – is payable where it can be shown that a letter was damaged or lost in the post due to the fault of the Post Office, its employees or agents. In order to provide evidence that an item has been posted, we advise you to obtain a certificate of posting, available on request and free of charge, when you post a letter or parcel at a post office counter.

Compensation is limited to the market value of goods lost or reduction in value of goods damaged. It will not be paid for money, monetary items or jewellery, nor for inadequately packed articles.

No legal liability to pay compensation exists in the ordinary overseas post, but insured services, which give compensation for loss or damage are available for letters and parcels.

Registration. This service is available for first-class post. It provides evidence of posting, a signature on delivery and special handling arrangements throughout. Compensation is payable for loss or damage, but not exceeding the market value, at various levels according to the registration fee paid. For an additional fee, compensation cover against consequential loss can also be arranged.

Recorded delivery is an optional extra facility available for a small fee with first- or second-class letters. It provides evidence of posting and a signature on delivery. Recorded delivery letters are ordinary unregistered letters with no special handling or compensation arrangements.

Parcels

There is a single national rate for sending parcels within the UK and to the Isle of Man and Channel Islands. Full details are available at Post Office Counters.

Special arrangements for businesses

The maximum parcel post weight is 25kg. If you post more than 1,000 parcels per year, you may qualify for a parcel contract with the Royal Mail. Contract holders can dispense with weighing parcels, sticking on stamps or using postage meters. The Post Office can also arrange collection of the parcels from your business premises. For further details, contact your Postal Sales Representative.

Cash-on-delivery service

This service is available within the UK and from the UK to the Channel Islands and the Isle of Man, but not to the Irish Republic. You can send the following items in the service with an invoice value of up to £30: ordinary parcels; compensation fee parcels; registered packets.

The Post Office collects payment and passes it on to the sender; invoice values over £50 are only collected on Post Office premises.

Postage forward parcel service

This service is designed to meet the needs of trading organizations who wish to obtain a parcel from a customer without putting him or her to the expense of paying the postage. The customer is sent an unstamped addressed label, wrapper or container with a special design. The design may be incorporated in newspaper advertisements or other publications for use as an address label. The parcel is posted in the ordinary way but without a stamp, and the addressee pays the charges on all such parcels he or she receives. The service does not operate to the Isle of Man, the Channel Islands or the Irish Republic.

Compensation

The ordinary inland parcel service is not designed as a compensation service, but limited compensation is payable where it can be shown that a parcel was lost or damaged in the post due to the fault of the Post Office, its employees or agents. You are strongly urged in your own interests and in those of the addressee to obtain a Certificate of Posting and keep it safe so that it will be available as evidence of posting if you should need to make a claim for compensation. If you wish to send articles of greater value the compensation fee parcel service should be used. Whichever service is used, compensation will be limited to the market value of the item lost, or to the reduction in value of items damaged. Compensation is not payable in certain circumstances.

Compensation fee (CF) parcels

A parcel for an address in Great Britain, Northern Ireland, the Channel Islands or the Isle of Man may be sent as a CF parcel. You may also send a CF parcel by the cash-on-delivery service. Compensation is payable for a parcel lost or damaged in the post within certain limits according to the fee paid. There is no special handling or security treatment en route. No compensation can be paid for damage to inadequately packed articles. There is no compensation for money or certain monetary articles sent in CF parcels. Full details of this service are given in the *Post Office Guide*.

SuperService

A business to business consignment service, offering guaranteed 48-hour delivery. It is designed for high-volume business customers whose annual use of the service will add up to more than £10,000.

SuperService provides free confirmation of delivery, a detailed weekly service report, and free insurance for loss or damage of up to £1,000 for each parcel. Full details can be obtained from local Royal

Mail Parcels sales representatives by calling Freephone 0800 300-363.

Newspapers and magazines

Newspapers and magazines distributed by post

Copies of publications including any supplements which have been registered as newspapers at the Post Office may be sent by the inland newspaper post and are given the same service as first-class letters. The publications must be specially posted by the publishers, printers or agents. All other newspapers are transmitted as first- or second-class letters according to the postage paid.

There is a small fee payable for registration as a newspaper. For details of this and newspaper and magazine postage rates, see the *Post Office Guide*.

Special Services

Datapost

Datapost offers a fast, timetabled, guaranteed, door-to-door delivery service for goods and documents. Delivery is guaranteed by 10am next day to main business centres and by noon to almost everywhere else.

Datapost can handle individual items of up to 30kg within the UK. There is no limit to the total weight of a consignment. The service offers free insurance for loss or damage to goods of up to £5,000 and from £100 to £10,000 for any consequential loss incurred through damage or delay. Special arrangements are available for high-volume users, and contract customers can also save money by using specially priced pre-paid Datapost packs.

Datapost collections can be arranged by making a free call on 0800 88 44 22. Alternatively packages can be handed in at any of the 3,000 post offices nationwide that accept Datapost.

Royal Mail Special Delivery

This service is available with first-class letters for an extra fee and provides accelerated treatment at the delivery office. If a special delivery letter is not delivered on the first working day after posting – provided that it was posted in time to achieve this – the fee is automatically refunded to the sender.

Intelpost

Intelpost is a high speed electronic mail service for the transmission of documents within the UK and to overseas destinations.

Customers can link into the Intelpost system, using compatible facsimile equipment or telex, or hand in material at any of the designated Intelpost Post Offices in the UK. It can then be transmitted to selected post offices throughout the UK or to destinations in more than 30 overseas countries, where documents can be picked up during normal hours or delivered by messenger.

Outgoing mail services

The Post Office provides a number of collection services, some free and others at varying fees, depending upon whether the collection is made in town or in the country and on the number and frequency of letters or parcels collected.

Incoming mail services

Redirection

This service is invaluable if you are moving to a new business or private address. Redirection may be initially for a period of one, three or twelve months and may be prolonged for a further period of up to twelve months. The fees for redirection are relatively small in comparison to the inconvenience of having your mail go astray.

Delivery at another address (diversion)

For an annual fee, you can have mail which is addressed to your business address delivered to your private address or *vice versa*. Similarly, mail can be diverted from one branch of your business to another.

Retention of postal packets

If you do not want your mail to be delivered, the Post Office will retain it for a fee for a period of up to two months. There is no charge for retention up to five weeksdays at Christmas and Easter, or up to three weekdays during the Spring or late Summer Bank Holidays. This service is intended for business premises and is available for residential premises only in exceptional circumstances.

A variety of other incoming mail services may be provided on request or by special arrangement.

Miscellaneous

Miscellaneous postal services include pre-stamped inland and over-seas stationery, lightweight self-sealing packs with air-filled linings to protect the contents, strong card boxes for parcels, and a variety of special supplies and services for the philatelist.

Overseas services

The major services include:
Letters and postcards. Primarily for correspondence, although goods up to 2 kg may be sent as letters.
Printed papers Full Rate. For printed matter of a non-literary nature, such as catalogues and advertising.
Printed papers Reduced Rate. For books, newspapers, etc.
Small Packets. For small quantities of goods.
Parcels. For goods up to 20 kg to most countries with a choice of speed and price.
Swiftair. An express airmail letter service available to all parts of the world.

Services aimed particularly at the business user include:
Airstream. Designed for companies sending regular quantities of letters and printed material abroad. It offers the speed of airmail and a simple charging system through bulk weighing. Pre-sorted contract services for bulk posters of printed papers are available.
Accelerated surface post. is a pre-sort contract service for printed papers, using air transport for speed combined with surface trans-port for economy.
Surface Printed Paper Contract. For bulk quantities of magazines and periodicals which do not need the urgency of Acclerated Surface Post.
Direct Agents Bag Service. A worldwide non-contract service for customers who regularly send large numbers of printed papers by a surface route to a single address.
International Direct Mail. For businesses which want to target mailshots at overseas customers.
International Business Reply Service. The service operates to a number of European countries and the United Arab Emirates and allows businesses to enclose reply-paid cards or envelopes in their mailings. The business in the UK pays a standard fee for each reply received and an annual licence fee.

Datapost International offers a fast guaranteed service to over 100 countries. It forms part of a major multinational network – EMS – providing speedy, secure delivery.

The service provides next-day delivery for documents to many European countries; merchandise takes 48 hours. For countries like Malaysia, Singapore and Taiwan delivery is within three to four days. Goods up to 20kg can be carried to most destinations and there is no limit on the total weight of a consignment. There is a money back guarantee if goods are not delivered on time, free insurance of up to £5,000 for damage or loss of goods and from £100 to £10,000 cover for consequential loss.

Goods can be handed in at 3,000 post offices throughout the country or a collection arranged by making a free call on 0800 88 44 22.

Customs and VAT requirements

All goods sent abroad by post, whether in letter packets, small packets or parcels, must be declared to Customs on special forms. These are available from post offices or as packs (complete with invoices, VAT labels and a Certificate of Posting) from:

Sitpro Ltd, Customer Service, Freepost, London SW1Y 6BR

Formecon Services Ltd., Douglas House, Gateway, Crewe CW1 1YN.

Goods exported by post are exempt from VAT, but to claim exemption exporters have to assure Customs that goods have actually been put in the post. Each item valued at over £10 must have a VAT label, available from VAT offices, and Customs will require a Certificate of Posting as proof of export. All loose documents should be placed in an adhesive envelope and securely taped to the parcel. These are available from post offices or Formecon Services, or from:

Tenza Tapes Ltd, Carlton Park Industrial Estate, Mail Road, Carlton, Saxmundham Suffolk IP17 2NL

Please consult the *Post Office Guide* for full details of eligibility of contents, methods of packing, size limits, dangerous substances etc.

2

Abbreviations and foreign words

There is more than one form of shorthand (see Chapter 47). The best way to shorten correspondence is often to use abbreviations. Sometimes these are quaintly English or even Anglo-Saxon in origin. Sometimes they have crept in from foreign tongues – which, on occasion, provide expressions for which there is no useful English equivalent.

Here is a list of abbreviations and foreign terms in common use. These are culled from a vast numbers, so if the initials which follow your name are not included do not be offended. The list is a random sample for your use.

a/c   account
ack   acknowledge
ad hoc   for this occasion
ad idem   as one, e.g. the minds of contract makers
a fortiori   even more so; with added force
alter ego   'other self'
amicus curiae   friend of the court; generally, counsel who appears out of courtesy to the court and not representing a client
ante meridiem   before noon
ARIBA   Associate of the Royal Institute of British Architects
au fait   fully conversant (or expert) in a matter

BA   Bachelor of Arts
BC   Before Christ
BCom   Bachelor of Commerce
BD   Bachelor of Divinity
BM   Bachelor of Medicine
BMA   British Medical Association
bona fide   in good faith
BSc   Bachelor of Science

BSI   British Standards Institution
Bt, Bart   Baronet
Cantab.   of Cambridge University
CB   Commander of the Order of the Bath
CBE   Commander of the Order of the British Empire
CBI   Confederation of British Industry

c/f   carried forward
cif   cost insurance freight
C-in-C   Commander-in-Chief
CMG   Companion of the Order of St Michael and St George
c/o   care of
COD   cash on delivery
contra   against
Cr   credit or creditor
Cx   contrast

DBE   Dame of the Order of the British Empire
DD   Doctor of Divinity
DDS   Doctor of Dental Surgery
de facto   in fact (often as opposed to *de jure*)
de jure   in law, as a matter of law
de novo   again, anew
ditto   the same
Dr   Doctor;

E & OE   errors and ommissions excepted
e.g.   *exempli gratia;* for example
enc.   enclosure
ex   from or out of

FAI   Fellow of Auctioneers Institute
FIPM   Fellow of the Institute of Personnel Management
fob   free on board
for   free on rail
FRCP   Fellow of the Royal College of Physicians
FRCS   Fellow of the Royal College of Surgeons
FRIBA   Fellow of the Royal Institute of British Architects

GC   George Cross
GM   George Medal

HE   His or Her Excellency or Eminence
HM   His or Her Majesty (or Majesty's)

Hon.   The Honourable
HRH   His or Her Royal Highness

i.e.,   *id est;* that is
Inc.   Incorporated; – US equivalent of Ltd. or plc
in flagrante   caught in the act
IOU   I owe you

JP   Justice of the Peace

k   £1,000
KB   Knight of the Bath;   Knight Bachelor
KCB   Knight Commander of the Bath
KCMG   Knight Commander of the Order of St Michael and St George

LL.B.   Bachelor of Laws
LL.M.   Master of Laws

mala fide   in bad faith
MD   Doctor of Medicine; Managing Director
modus operandi   a method of operation or plan of working
MP   Member of Parliament
MRSA   Member of the Royal Society of Arts

nem.con.   no one voting against
non seq.   *non sequitur;* something that does not follow

o/d   overdraft or overdrawn
OHMS   On Her Majesty's Service
Oxon.   of Oxford University

PhD   Doctor of Philosophy
plc   public limited company
pm   *post meridiem;* afternoon
P.M.   post-mortem; after death
pp   *per procurationem;* on behalf of
Pres.   President
prima facie   at first glance
Prof.   Professor
PS   postscript
PTO   please turn over

QC   Queen's Counsel
Q.E.D   *quod erat demonstrandum;* which was to be demonstrated, i.e. we have proved that which we set out to prove

qv   *quod vide*; which see

RA   Royal Artillery;   Royal Academician
RAF   Royal Air Force
RSVP   *repondez s'il vous plait*; please answer
rtd or rd   refer to drawer
Rt Hon.   Right Honourable
Rt Revd.   Right Reverend

seriatim   serially, point by point
sine die   without another date being fixed; indefinitely
sine qua non   something without which you cannot manage, hence a necessity
SMP   Statutory Maternity Pay
SSP   Statutory Sick Pay
status quo   existing situation
stet   let it stand, normally to restore words which have been crossed out
sub judice   under consideration by the court

TUC   Trades Union Congress

ultra vires   beyond the powers (usually of a company or court)

vade-mecum   something which should go with you always; a regular companion
verbatim   word for word
Very Revd   Very Reverend (as to Dean)
v.   vide; see
viz.   *videlicet*; namely
VP   Vice-President

∴   therefore
=   equals
≠   does not equal
>   greater than
<   less than

3
Style – and the press

Writers sometimes poke fun at 'journalese'. This is a mistake. Journalists are trained to use words accurately, precisely and with economy. Their newspapers often have 'house rules' specifying the style, punctuation and terminology to be used or abhorred. These are commonly contained in a 'style book'.

Here are some hints which commercial letterwriters would do well to note – although some are matters of taste, rather than rules of letterwriting law.

Style should at all times be aimed at achieving accuracy, clarity and readability. It should also be authoritative. Remember that if *you* don't understand a phrase, few readers will. Check and recheck and never take a chance and leave it in.

Adjectives, overuse of

Too many adjectives defeat their own purpose. Simplicity is the keynote of good style and any word that is not doing a job is superfluous.

Spelling – American and British

Many Americanisms have become absorbed into the English language, such as 'teenage', 'commuter', 'babysitter'. Others have not and should be avoided.

Anglicized words

Many foreign words, too, have become accepted English usage and require no special treatment. But it may be necessary to keep the accents on some French words.

Capitals

Avoid too many capitals. The fashion now is to knock them down, except for abbreviations or specific references – for example, 'Lower Biggleswade's Health Committee' at the first mention, but subsequently 'the committee' or 'health committee'. The Government is always capped if specifically the British; not, if not.

Collective nouns

These take a singular verb. Not 'The Health Committee/Government are' but 'The Health Committee/Government is'. Again there are obvious exceptions. You cannot, for example, say 'The police is', though you could say 'The police force is'.

Long words

Avoid long and pompous words where there are good shorter equivalents – for example, 'send' not 'despatch', 'about' not 'concerning', 'need' not 'necessity'.

Mixed metaphors

Don't mix them. (See also Chapter 18.)

Paragraphing

The look of the page is aided by good paragraphing. It adds horizontal to vertical space. New thoughts need new paragraphs.

Punctuation

Curb the tendency to over-punctuate. Punctuation is only an aid to sense. Too many commas and full stops merely confuse. Three short sentences are better than one which contains a number of subsidiary clauses.

Quotes

Modern practice is for direct quotation to be carried in single quotes. For example, he said, 'Listen to me.' If the speaker is reporting what someone else has said, then it's double quotes inside single quotes. For example, he said, 'When I spoke to her, she said, "Listen to me!".' Which style you use is, of course, a matter for you.

Hyphens

Words like today, midday, tomorrow, no one, are never hyphenated. ('No one' is not one word but two.)

Slang

Slang words are rarely acceptable but there are exceptions. Some words which were once slang are now vernacular. Others are borderline.

Index